NAKED MANAGEMENT

BARE ESSENTIALS FOR MOTIVATING THE X-GENERATION AT WORK

Marc Muchnick, Ph.D.

St. Lucie Press
Delray Beach, Florida

Printed and bound in the U.S.A. Printed on acid-free paper.
10 9 8 7 6 5 4 3 2 1

ISBN: 1-57444-061-6

S^{t}L

Published by
St. Lucie Press
100 E. Linton Blvd., Suite 403B
Delray Beach, Florida
(407) 274-9906
(407) 274-9927

DEDICATION

This book is dedicated to the following amazing people:

My beautiful wife Kimmy,
who inspires me
through her love,
smiles,
laughter,
and unconditional support;

My dearest grandfathers Ben Muchnick and Mel Schoenfeld,
both of whom genuinely knew
the power of the human spirit
and who spent their lives helping others
discover It;

And my good friend Andy "The Suss" Sussman,
who died an X'er at age 28,
and whose vivid memory
will forever give me "the attitude"
when I need it most.
Hats off to you, Suss.

TABLE OF CONTENTS

ABOUT THE AUTHOR

Marc H. Muchnick, Ph.D. is an innovative leader in the field of organizational and human behavior. His depth of experience as a trainer, management consultant, educator, and researcher provide him with a unique perspective on current industry trends and human resource development issues. Muchnick earned his Ph.D. in Organizational Psychology and Master's degree in Clinical Psychology from the California School of Professional Psychology at San Diego, and holds a B.A. in Business Psychology from the University of Texas at Austin's prestigious Plan II Honors Program. He began his professional career working for Ken Blanchard, internationally renowned for co-authoring *The One Minute Manager*.

Dr. Muchnick's organizational training and development firm, People First Group, features speaking engagements, customized seminars, and comprehensive consulting services on managing and motivating Generation X, leadership effectiveness, customer service, communication skills, team building, and other high-demand topics. He also serves as a professor for Nova Southeastern University's Business and Administrative Studies Program in South Florida, Jamaica, and the Bahamas, where he teaches one of the world's first management courses on Generation X. His professional affiliations include Phi Beta Kappa, the American Society for Training and Development, and Big Brothers of America.

Muchnick has facilitated projects for major corporations including Trusthouse Forte Hotels, Dean Witter Reynolds, General Dynamics, Jiffy Lube, Kinko's, Symbiosis, and Siemens; and has produced numerous widely distributed training materials. In addition, leading companies such as United Airlines, NationsBank, PepsiCo, The Ritz-Carlton Hotels, Office Depot, The Levy Restaurants, Mirage Resorts, The Home Depot, Dryclean-U.S.A., and Tulane University have worked closely with him on making *Naked Management* a success. Dr. Muchnick and his wife Kim — both Generation X'ers — reside in Boca Raton, Florida.

# ACKNOWLEDGEMENTS

I would particularly like to thank the following positive people in my life:

My parents, for everything and then some;
Mo, for stepping up to the plate and clearing the lane;
Adam & Cindy, for their help;
Drs. Mark & Maxine Rossman;
Rog, Slick, Rye, & Johnny Lou;
the Grammies & the Scruff;
Alan & Marci, Debbie & Karl, Chayks & Chayks, Joann & Steve, Ad & Jen;
Shengie, Q, Junior, Whitey & Lisa, Portland Karen & Steve,
Brett, Tim & Angelle;
The Shanks, William "Little Bro" Moreland, Fox-boy, Adam #3 & Cheryl,
Mitch & Jamie;
Claire & Steve, The Mnookens, Ira, Schwedel, Elon, Doc Tesone,
Jim & Judy G., Terry A.;
Dennis & Dennis, Drew, Ann, Stephanie, and the rest of the great
St. Lucie Press team;
All of the super X'ers and non-X'ers quoted in this book
(some of whose identities have been protected);
And each one of the high-quality companies and individuals featured
in the X'er Success Stories.

A special inspirational thanks to Jerry, gone to where the water
tastes like wine.

INTRODUCTION

Why would anyone write a management book these days when the shelves at every bookstore are stuffed with the latest bandwagon revelations on reengineering, customer service, team building, working smarter not harder, excellence this and that, TQM, and every imaginable spin on the quality movement which has no end? Thousands of self-proclaimed gurus regurgitate the same rhetoric and spit it out in their own secret-recipe jargon which often is outdated by the time it hits the mass market. Who, with clear conscience, can step into that lion pit and declare they have discovered the Missing Management Link, a kernel of truth which somehow got overlooked?

With these thoughts in mind, I wrote*Naked Management: Bare Essentials for Motivating the X-Generation at Work* because it is timely, unique, and urgently needed. My mission is not to suggest that I have found a set of human behavior principles which have never been heard of before. Instead, I draw from a fundamental motivation theory base that already exists and apply it to a significant workplace problem which until now has lacked a practical, clearly spelled-out solution.

The tangible result of my efforts — supported by more than 1,000 interviews conducted over the past several years with managers and X'ers throughout the world, in addition to my own experiences and personal findings as a training manager, human resource development consultant, university professor, and full-time X'er — is *Naked Management. Naked Management* (a) provides managers and company leaders with an invaluable five-point NAKED Model for conquering motivational problems with younger employees, the "X-generation," and (b) outlines the critical responsibilities that both managers and members of this X-workforce have in making the utilization of the NAKED Model successful.

Naked Management delivers the three components that practical managers as well as X'ers seek in a management approach: it is user-friendly, measurable, and useful when applied. Personal application "X'ercises" are provided in each chapter, while handy "Naked Checklists" (for managers and X'ers) and informative slice-of-life success profiles from top companies follow major learning sections. There is not a lot of fluff in this book; only instant utility and a critical path to success.

The following are several frequently asked questions regarding *Naked Management.* My responses are designed to provide up-front clarification as well as a contextual framework for readers:

WHO IS GENERATION X?

X'ers are members of a generation that is collectively saying "no" to traditional management approaches in the workplace. They are the product of latch-key parenting and unprecedented divorce rates. Their inheritance has been a stagnant job market, corporate downsizing, and limited wage mobility. In terms of their future, they feel abandoned, cheated, and left to fend for themselves. They are the first generation predicted to earn less than their parents did.

According to Neil Howe and Bill Strauss in *13th Generation,* X'ers are considered those individuals whose birth years range from 1961-1981. X'ers are, based on this estimate, close to 80 million strong in America alone — this parallels the size of the Baby Boom generation. Consequently, Generation X is a significant and viable force in the labor pool. Eighty percent of all entry-level new hires in virtually every industry — banking, retail, legal, medical, technical, computer, sales, hotel and restaurant, airline, etc. — are currently sourced from the X-Generation. This trend will only continue throughout this decade and into the twenty-first century.

HOW DO MANAGERS VIEW GENERATION X'ERS?

In light of the context in which Generation X'ers have grown up, they are most popularly known for their shortcomings. Terminology such as "slackers," "whiners," and "underachievers" is commonly used to describe X'ers. Just a stereotype? Perhaps much of what is said about Generation X is simply media hype. But there are countless managers and company owners, even those who are X'ers themselves, who feel the X-Generation has earned its negative stigma. After spending years climbing organizational ladders and working hard to get ahead, they see X'ers as lazy complainers who do not want to pay their dues. They resent the "this world owes me" mentality they find characteristic of X'ers in general. Their advice to Generation X: get a real work ethic or get out of my face.

However, what managers and corporate leaders are now realizing, regardless of their perception of X'ers, is that rinsing their hands of the X-Generation is not a plausible option. Due to the overwhelming and growing population of X'ers in the ranks and an ever-increasing number of X'ers in management positions, the fate of companies and Generation X are inevitably intertwined. Turnover, absenteeism, productivity, sales, efficiency, quality, morale, and cost savings are just a sampling of the critical bottom-line issues at stake.

WHAT IS THIS "NAKED MODEL" AND HOW IS IT DESIGNED TO BE USED?

In essence, the million-dollar question facing anyone who manages Generation X'ers is how to effectively motivate them at work. It is a definite and very real challenge. In *Naked Management,* I propose the NAKED Model as a practical and user-friendly tool for reducing X'er turnover, increasing X'er productivity, and boosting X'er morale and job commitment.

The thrust of the NAKED Model is to make a gut-level connection with the X-Generation workforce. It is the foundation of *Naked Management,* and geared toward facilitating a positive, bare-boned, and implicitly genuine working relationship with X'ers. The five components of the NAKED Model, clearly grounded in basic motivational theory, are designed to be used *together* as an integrated concept. These dimensions represent the core of what X'ers deem to be the essential aspects of work: autonomy, involvement, recognition, understanding, and feedback.

SO WHY JUST X'ERS?

While the focus of *Naked Management* is on motivating Generation X, it can certainly work well with any group of employees. So why target X'ers? The stark reality is that not only are members of the X-Generation here to stay, but they will not tolerate the typical "old school" boss that prior generations have known — and still know — so well. Most X'ers would rather quit, or are in the process of leaving, jobs where their managers use an autocratic, top-down, "jump-when-I-say-jump" supervisory style. In addition, despite a groundswell of "total quality," "empowerment," and "upside-down pyramid" jargon in corporate America, the majority of Generation X agrees that there is too much lip service and too many hollow promises when it comes to actually shifting paradigms and "walking the talk."

Yes, *Naked Management* makes sense to X'ers and non-X'ers alike. But a key difference is that the X-Generation demands it. Failing to consistently implement each of the five NAKED Model points with X'ers can ultimately bring a company to its knees, if not kill it, through rampant turnover, excessive rehiring costs, employee theft and sabotage, stifled productivity, and depleted morale. Non-X'ers, on the other hand, are more apt to find a way to accept (or at least endure) authoritarian, controlling, power-wielding, and insensitive managers. Perhaps this is because they have more at stake than most X'ers, or they have been oversensitized to the status quo. In any case, *Naked Management* is a business necessity in every company where X'ers work.

HOW CAN NAKED MANAGEMENT BE A TWO-WAY STREET?

Without mutual responsibility, any effort to make a connection with Generation X'ers and hence, to motivate them, is futile. A striking aspect of *Naked Management* is that for every NAKED Model point, there are a set of prescribed actions for managers *and* X'ers to take. Thus, *Naked Management* requires dual participation. Because both managers and employees have mandated roles in its implementation, personal buy-in and a sense of joint ownership for progress and success are increased.

Marc H. Muchnick, Ph.D.
Boca Raton, Florida

A WORD ON NAKED MANAGEMENT AND TEAM MEMBER DIVERSITY

Naked Management is blind
to color
creed
cultural background
ethnicity
gender
hairstyle
height
nationality
physical and mental challenges
race
sexual orientation
shoe size
and weight.

The principles of Naked Management
apply to *everyone* in today's diverse workforce —
employers and employees,
managers and staff members,
X'ers and non-X'ers.

Implementing the NAKED Model
means respecting the needs and feelings
of all individuals,
and finding effective methods
for including each of them in
the Naked Management process.

NAKED TERMINOLOGY

Getting Naked: the process of stripping away layers of resentment, staving off the inclination to point the finger and squelching any desire to manipulate, dominate, or sabotage others.

Naked Contract: an agreement between managers and X'ers regarding their individual responsibilities and performance goals.

Naked Frame of Mind: the positive mental state achieved when managers and X'ers concentrate on the utility of each other's special qualities as opposed to getting caught up in the negative dynamics of their inherent differences.

Naked Management: a timely, practical, and hands-on approach to managing members of the X-Generation in the workplace by effectively using the five-point NAKED Model.

NAKED Model: the five key components of Naked Management theory.

Naked Moment: a brief but awe-inspiring experience which results from a manager's skillful application of the NAKED model.

Naked Tracking System: a measurement tool for tracking the ongoing progress and effectiveness of Naked Management applications.

Over-X-tended: when managers feel pushed beyond acceptable limits to meet X'er needs and demands.

Stripping: see "Getting Naked."

Under-X-pended: when X'ers feel utilized far below their personal potential and capabilities.

X-Crisis: a growing workplace dilemma characterized by X'erism (see "X'erism") from managers in the wake of their concern over diminished X'er motivation, performance, and attendance.

X'er: a member of the X-Generation.

X'ercise: a written exercise found at the end of each chapter in this book to stimulate active reader participation and thought with respect to presented topics.

X'erism: X'er-focused apathy and resentment, including the negative X'er generalizations, stereotypes, and attitudes one maintains.

X-Generation: generally considered those individuals whose birth years range from 1964-1976, although some definitions have been expanded to include the birth years 1961-1981.

X-workforce: X'ers who have joined or who potentially will join the current workforce.

X-workplace: the market arena characterized by businesses and organizations which provide jobs for X'ers.

1

THE X-CRISIS

Top Ten Complaints About the X-Workforce

10. Lazy — real underachievers.
9. Look to "Melrose Place" for answers to social crises.
8. Try to buck the system — don't want to pay their dues.
7. Big-time whiners.
6. Are all high on dope or something.
5. No concept of where they're going.
4. More concerned about watching Beavis and Butthead than finishing the job.
3. Lack team-player skills — just out for themselves.
2. Would rather be bungee jumping.
1. Too hung up on that grunge music.

Anonymous David Letterman Groupie

CRISIS AT A GLANCE

"Those X-Generation kids. They put on quite a convincing show in the interview, and then poof! They're gone within nine months, at best two years."

Margaret, 44 — Associate director of regional sales for electronics superstores in Dallas, TX

"X'ers are actually naive enough to think they can start their new job one day and be in line for department head two months later."

Tim, 38 — district manager for expanding convenience store chain in Minneapolis, MN

"I've got a bottom line to meet, see. If I spend my time baby-sitting and worrying about all the various problems that face this generation, we'll never be profitable.

Those who can't take the heat of a real job should go back to the french-fry pit."

Alex, 40 — managing director of casino operations in Las Vegas, NV

How do managers motivate members of the X-Generation? Thus far, there have been no definitive answers. In fact, many managers feel that the X-workforce — the new and culturally diverse labor pool predominantly made up of today's teens and twenty-somethings — poses one of the greatest human resource challenges of the century. Naked Management addresses this quandary head-on.

First, the context in which Naked Management is most applicable must be defined. X'ers typically have been stereotyped as "lost," "slackers," and "lazy," and are often characterized by employers as the most unprepared, uncooperative, and underachieving generation in history. Many managers who have spent years inching their way up company ladders are appalled by what they view as X-Generation nonconformity, non-sticktuitiveness, and sheer disinterest in playing by the rules when it comes to cultivating a strong work ethic. They stand firm in their "X'erism" — the negative generalizations, stereotypes, and attitudes they maintain about X'ers.

Managers who harbor a high level of X'erism, (some of them X'ers themselves), are not shy about expressing their views regarding the X-workforce:

"For X'ers it's just a job, not a career. If it doesn't get done today, no problem — it'll get done tomorrow or maybe the day after that. Basically, their work ethic is out to lunch. There's no dedication or commitment with these folks. Loyalty means that they're just here until something better comes along. A job to them is just money to pay their bills and bar tab."

Joe, 47 — food and beverage manager
at full-service hotel in Atlanta, GA

"The X-Generation expects a lot — I should know. But the X'ers who work for me expect too much. Their motto is 'give me a lot more money and let me do a lot less work.' Employment is like a social club for them. So how do you win as a young manager? These are my peers."

Alicia, 28 — retail clothing store
assistant manager in major indoor
shopping mall in Scottsdale, AZ

On the other side of this classic "we-they" conflict, X'ers resent being lumped into a category (see Figure 1). They become upset when they are labeled as one homogeneous group, especially if it carries a negative stigma. Ironically, the terms "X'er" and "X-Generation" are inherently nontainted and arbitrary. In modern algebraic thought, "x" represents *all* possibilities within a given domain. Naked Management helps to promote this latent objectivity by providing both managers and X'ers with a viable, nonjudgmental paradigm for working together.

Top Ten Rebuttals to Complaints About the X-Workforce

10. Slogan "Proud to be a Workaholic" doesn't sell anymore.
9. Did you say Burger Shack was hiring?
8. Just put it on my social insecurity deduction.
7. Gee, human sacrifice *is* the way things get done around here.
6. Meet you in the layoff line.
5. Maybe if I jump through a few more hoops I'll get promoted to assistant fry cook.
4. Forty thousand dollars worth of student loan debt — no problem.
3. Oh, what a feeling! We're the first American generation ever predicted to do worse than our parents.
2. Wow, $4.65 an hour. That's almost enough for groceries and half the rent.
1. X *this!*

Anonymous X'er

Figure 1

THE ECONOMY FROM HELL

Question: What can be opened and closed, accessed only by a secret code, filled to no end, yet holds virtually nothing?
Answer: An X'ers bank account.

Times are not easy for young adults entering the workforce today. Popular terminology like "McJob" and "Slacker Work" have become commonplace for describing the employment opportunities readily available to the X-Generation, which often consist of fast-food counter jobs and shopping mall sales positions:

"A college degree doesn't mean you've got it made, X'er. Real-world experience is what matters. The job you thought you'd have right out of school was just a fantasy created in a four-color marketing brochure."

Dan, 51 — corporate headhunter in Stamford, CT

Unprecedented job cuts, a sluggish economy, falling real wages and abundant competition help constitute the perpetual Economy from Hell for X'ers. According to Nicholas Zill and John Robinson's American Demographics article, "Between 1983 and 1992, the median weekly earnings of young men aged 16 to 24 who were full-time workers fell 9 percent, from $314 per week to $285 per week in constant 1992 dollars. Over the same period, inflation-adjusted earnings of young women in the same age group slipped 4 percent, from $277 to $267 per week."

Plainly spoken, the majority of X'ers are finding it tough to get a decent job and survive on their own:

"Living paycheck to paycheck is fairly standard for most X'ers. Their credo is, 'live frugally and pray to God the economy turns around.' However, 'buckle up — we're about to make a crash landing' wouldn't be too far off the mark either, I'm afraid."

Vicki, 41 — reservations center customer service manager in Memphis, TN

"The problem today is that there are too many young people like me: college-educated, hard-working, but can't find a real job. Fifty thousand dollars of student loan debt and look where it got me — mixing cocktails and calling cabs for drunks."

Bob, 23 — bartender in upper West Side of New York, NY

"No wonder so many of us still live with our folks. I predict my generation will quickly find itself submerged in a dual economic misery: we will either join the petty bourgeois working class as robotic slaves to corporate America or platoon ourselves into the realm of riffraff scum after failed attempts to hawk our own wares."

Tommy, 22 — temporarily unemployed, has held 11 part-time jobs in Fort Lauderdale, FL

Company downsizing (coined as "rightsizing" by many marketing opportunists) is a significant contributor to the Economy from Hell. The trend toward major corporate mergers, full-scale reengineering and massive layoffs not only impacts the X-workforce financially, but psychologically as well. The omnipresence of these issues results in a general mistrust of employers and the notion of job security itself. In many organizations, the sacrifice for achieving profitability has been telling loyal employees with decades of tenure to hit the road. To X'ers, the inferred moral is that they cannot trust anyone these days, especially their employers:

"People come and go around here. I don't think top management really cares one way or another who does the work, as long as it gets done. Regardless of how long you've been here or how much effort you've given, when your time's up, it's up. I call it job insecurity. It's why I spend at least one lunch hour per week networking and interviewing with other firms."

Sarah, 29 — accountant at large consulting firm in Portland, OR

"What my generation faces is more than just the basic challenge of becoming mature adults. It is the essence of trying to survive in a brutal job market. And when you do find a job, it's either low wages, no benefits, over-demanding managers, or all of the above."

Maria, 27 — office "temp" at property management firm in Austin, TX

Critics have cause to assert that members of the X-Generation are not bashful about putting themselves first. X'ers, in their quest to establish careers, feel that self-preservation is essential. A stark implication from the Economy from Hell is that the X-workforce — the core applicant pool for the next decade or so — will maintain a substantial amount of mistrust, self-concern, short-term focus, negativity, and doubt. This poses real problems for managers, and a challenge that is both sobering and certain.

OVER-X-TENDED, UNDER-X-PENDED

Following are two sides of a typical X-Crisis situation in the workplace:

"Six months ago Richard waltzes in here with a cocky attitude and I think to myself, maybe this guy has the confidence we're looking for out in the field. We pay him for his training and give him fair benefits. So why does he complain about every policy and procedure? Why does he always try to bend the rules?"

Paula, 41 — territory supervisor for beer and wine distributing company in St. Louis, MO

"If Paula would get off my case, I think things would be a lot better. It may come as a surprise to her that everything doesn't have to happen by the book. I may be young, but I have a lot of good ideas. My biggest gripe about this job is that my boss doesn't care what I think. I need a manager who values me."

Richard, 24 — sales representative, (works for Paula)

A striking aspect of the X-Crisis is the contrast in perceptions each party maintains. On one hand, managers feel they do more than their share to meet the needs of the X-Generation, while on the other hand, X'ers feel stifled by their managers. Most members of the X-workforce contend that managers generally fall short of meeting their expectations.

Given both perspectives, the resulting profile of the X-Crisis depicts a major schism. Managers feel "over-X-tended," or pushed beyond acceptable limits to meet X'er needs and demands. They see themselves as having gone the extra mile to accommodate X'ers, often at the expense of their personal time and departmental budgets. The X-workforce, in their opinion, takes them for granted and fails to appreciate their effort and good intentions. Members of the X-Generation, however, feel "under-X-pended," or utilized far below their personal potential and capabilities:

> *"Give a little? All's I do is give, pay my dues, and play the game. At the end of the day, I fight the realization that I'm going nowhere."*
>
> James, 26 — frontline associate at home improvement store in Omaha, NE

> *"My boss thinks I don't care because I don't stay late every night like he does. What he seems to forget is that I put in overtime whenever we need to make a tight deadline or when someone else needs help."*
>
> Susan, 19 — product development specialist at agricultural technology firm in Greensboro, NC

> *"If you tell me that I made a mistake, I'll work harder than anyone to make it right. But if you try to take away my self-esteem in the process, I'll shut down."*
>
> Denise, 23 — food expediter at South-western-style cafe in Santa Fe, NM

X'ers are confident that they have a lot to offer an organization if they are given respect and the chance to shine. Unfortunately, many managers find that when they *do* try to meet these needs, X'ers take advantage of them. The issues which invariably prevent a simple reconciliation of the X-Crisis may also help to perpetuate it.

STUCK IN THE MUD

"We're on the road to nowhere
Come on inside
Takin' that ride to nowhere
We'll take that ride"

Talking Heads

"Nowhere" is a place both managers and X'ers know increasingly well. This X-Crisis abyss is a giant obstacle in the road, a barrier to improved productivity and morale. Being nowhere is like being stuck in the mud—wheels spinning, going no place. It is virtual gridlock: complete workplace immobility.

To the surprise of many company leaders, the rollout of full-scale total quality initiatives, canned management programs, and annual presentations by motivational speakers do not eliminate manager-X'er gridlock. What they find is that it takes a lot more than simply reshuffling the deck to make a marked difference in people's worklives:

> *"In order to meet this year's tighter budget, we had to cut back on training. The executive team was thrilled with the projected savings. Since then, we've had a lot of entry-level, 'X-Generation' workers quit because of what they said (in their exit interviews) was a lack of concern for their advancement needs. Now the company is faced with the costs of recruiting, hiring, and training new employees. These additional expenses far exceed the money we originally thought we were saving."*
>
> Nicole, 48 — director of training at shipping company's corporate office in Los Angeles, CA

Both managers and X'ers seem to agree that everyone loses when they relentlessly spin their wheels in the mud. Currently, the X-Crisis is so far from being a "win-win" situation. Some managers gradually accept poor morale as a given and fall back on authoritarian tactics to elicit desired X'er job performance. X'ers frequently quit under the premise that they deserve better:

"Finally, after almost a full year of working for a jerk manager, I decided to leave. It was such a relief to get away from all the yelling and screaming. The only thing I remember about that place is being treated like a subhuman. I felt like a new person once I left."

David, 25 — former mental health technician at psychiatric hospital in Miami, FL

Little resolution has come out of the X-Crisis in the workplace. It is much easier to figure out what X'ers like to spend money on (e.g., shoes, beer, automobiles, jeans) than to attempt to understand what motivates them at work. At the end of the day, there is greater recognition of a very real problem, but an absence of a practical, measurable solution. The toxic combination of growing X'erism, a "we-they" mentality, an Economy from Hell, over-X-tended managers, and under-X-pended X'ers has created a virtual workplace wasteland. Moving out of this X-Crisis mess serves as a focal point of Naked Management.

X'ERCISE 1: TESTING THE WATERS

DIRECTIONS

For Managers:

Take a few moments to assess your feelings about X'ers in the workplace. Please indicate whether you agree or disagree with each of the following 10 statements by marking an "x" in the appropriate column on the right-hand side of the page. Then follow the scoring instructions below and discuss your results with other managers and/or X'ers.

For X'ers:

Take a few moments to assess how *your manager* feels about X'ers in the workplace. Please indicate whether (s)he would agree or disagree with each of the following 10 statements by marking an "x" in the appropriate column on the right-hand side of the page. Then follow the scoring instructions below and discuss your results with other X'ers and/or managers.

	AGREE	DISAGREE
1. As a group, X'ers have a poorer work ethic than the generations before them.	______	______
2. X'ers have too idealistic an outlook on how long it should take to get promoted up the company ladder.	______	______
3. Most X'ers hired today will quit within a year.	______	______
4. Because X'er turnover is high, recruiting and training them tends to waste both time and money.	______	______
5. X'ers have unrealistic expectations about how the workplace should meet their needs.	______	______
6. It is more X'ers' responsibility to get what they want out of the workplace, and less management's job to provide it for them.	______	______

	Agree	Disagree
7. Adapting one's management style just for X'ersis taking things too far.	______	______
8. X'ers do a lot of unnecessary complaining about issues that every working generation has had to face.	______	______
9. The problems of the X-workforce have been exaggerated.	______	______
10. The term "lazy" fits X'ers in the sense that most of them are unmotivated to pay their dues in the workplace.	______	______

SCORING

Please count the number of statements for which you marked the *"agree"* column (above), then determine your (or your manager's) level of "X'erism"—the negative generalizations, stereotypes, and attitudes you (or [s]he) maintain about X'ers—according to the following scale:

0-2 Agrees	=	**Low** X'erism
3-5 Agrees	=	**Medium** X'erism
6-10 Agrees	=	**High** X'erism

2

GETTING NAKED

Top Ten Reasons to Manage Naked

10. Part of that working smarter thing.
9. Doesn't require setting world record for most meetings attended in a day.
8. Sheds new light on getting "lean and mean."
7. See eye-to-eye with X'ers — no foolin'.
6. Better than being a benchsitter.
5. Complies with politically correct agenda.
4. Eliminates desire to fire everyone under 30.
3. Gives you time to get your own work done.
2. What's the worst thing that can happen?
1. Gets results with a smile.

Managers with a Mission
Key Largo, FL

YOU MIGHT AS WELL STRIP

"Any attempt by managers to improve the motivational levels of their subordinates should be prefaced by a self-examination on the part of the managers themselves. Are they aware of their major strengths and their major limitations? Do they have a clear notion of their own wants, desires, and expectations from their jobs? Are their perceptions of themselves consistent with the perceptions others have of them? In short, before managers attempt to deal with others, they should have a clear picture of their own role in the organizational milieu."

Richard Steers and Lyman Porter in
Motivation and Work Behavior

Naked Management is not about wallowing in the stagnation of gridlock, but about achieving positive solutions to bottom-line X-workforce issues. It is a conscious decision to start fresh instead of floundering in the X-Crisis mud, a commitment to "get naked" as opposed to going nowhere. When managers and X'ers get naked (in the context of Naked Management), they strip away layers of resentment, stave off the inclination to point the finger at each other and squelch any desire to manipulate, dominate, or sabotage one another.

"Stripping," a synonymous term for getting naked, does *not* stipulate giving up one's values, life learnings, nor actual clothing. Instead, the focus is on removing the layers of "dust" which prevent the effective management and motivation of X'ers. For managers, the first step to getting naked is seeking self-awareness. Stripping away the cobwebs that accumulate in organizational life helps establish an unobstructed foundation for accepting and integrating Naked Management skills.

Noteworthy are the difficulties when managers get naked. The prospect of searching within for the agenda-free self can produce resistance, apathy, feelings of vulnerability, and even terror. The following advice comes from managers who have "taken it off" and lived to tell the tale:

"Swallow your pride every now and then. Just because you're the boss doesn't mean you have to be 'bossy.' Remember, once you weren't in charge. As it is said, 'let people grow their own wings, and soon you'll soar with them.'"

Michael, 53 — unit supervisor at large
department store in Seattle, WA

> *"What I learned the hard way is that I carry around a lot of baggage which is the result of what was preached to me: do what I say, when I say it, and don't ask me stupid questions. I had to come to terms with the kind of boss I was and the type of manager I wanted to be."*
>
> Fran, 42 — finance manager at data processing company in Richmond, VA

Guidelines for getting naked also apply to X'ers. They, too, must pull their weight to pave the way for Naked Management. X'ers must become an asset, not a hindrance, to the joint pursuit of improving worklife. Characteristically, members of the X-Generation have concrete notions about how things *should* be. Stripping for the *X*-workforce mandates self-examination of the inherent role they can play in controlling their workplace predicament and in promoting better relationships with their managers.

As most X'ers who get naked will agree, it is a matter of taking responsibility:

> *"There were a lot of things I took for granted when I got this position. In my mind, I would be shown how to do every aspect of my job. Instead, I got thrown straight into the fray the moment I signed my first timecard. No instructions, no training, and nowhere to hide."*
>
> Deborah, 24 — airport rental care agent in Denver, CO

For managers and X'ers alike, getting naked means looking inward. This stripping ritual helps create a highly conducive environment for making positive change and for attaining the bare-bones condition that is a vital precursor to Naked Management.

THE NAKED CHALLENGE

There once was a manager from Maine
Who saw morale getting washed down the drain.
"Nothing seems to work," he would cry,
Finally, one young staffer replied:
"Get to know us, there's a lot you can gain."

Greg, 46 — restaurant general manager, New Orleans, LA

Introspection is just half of the battle when it comes to getting naked. The real struggle is for managers and X'ers to go from basic self-awareness to a state of reciprocal acceptance. This process does not necessitate that everyone involved become best friends. Instead, people must sincerely try to acknowledge and respect the differences which tend to set them apart. Essentially, they must gain a more lucid view of what causes friction in their working relationship. The "naked" challenge, then, is for managers and X'ers to understand each other at a working level, using *that* as a framework for achieving mutual objectives.

With respect to getting to know the X-workforce, age is just one factor in the mix of variables which overlap to form what is distinctly X'er in nature. The unique attributes of this generation are anchored in their workplace values. While it would be naive to assume that there are no values which *both* managers and X'ers deem important, a set of X'er-specific core beliefs indeed exists. Not all X'ers possess the exact same values, but the majority of X'ers share a common value base which guides their behaviors and attitudes about work. The X-workforce value pool shown in Figure 2 was derived from interviews with a diverse cross-section of over 1,000 X'ers. Central components of this X'er value scheme are freedom/autonomy, involvement, recognition, empathy/understanding, and communication.

What is Important to X'ers At Work

Flexibility — Trust

Balance — Quality of Life

Feedback — Challenge

Freedom/Autonomy
Involvement
Recognition
Empathy/Understanding
Communication

Fun/Happiness — Education/Training

Honesty — Respect

Appreciation — Pride

Figure 2

Another discrete aspect of the X-workforce deals with their expectations and perceptions of the workplace. In an era where cutting entitlements is the trend, X'ers stand out as part of a generation which feels society owes it something. Whether at a conscious or subconscious level, X'ers want payback for the Economy from Hell. But as one X'er points out, this resolve is based more on concerns for equity than on hatred of everyone over the age of 40:

> *"It's not about blame, it's about justice. My generation would like to believe that the economic mayhem we find ourselves squirming in is the fault of short-sided, impulsive baby boomers. Yet while everyone searches for an oversimplified explanation to this complex state of affairs, the dismal reality remains the same for us. The thing we're truly upset about is that life doesn't match up to what the advertisements said."*
>
> Bill, 26 — savings and loan teller in Kansas City, MO

Instant return on investment summarizes many X'ers' expectations of work. This means they want up-front respect and a fast track. They refuse to be treated like second-class citizens. Most X'ers cringe when they hear that their career growth is limited because times are tough and there is nowhere to move up, or how job mobility is a fantasy in the world of cutbacks and monolithic mergers. They believe it is their given right to step into the saddle and blaze forward. It is not uncommon for X'ers straight out of school to walk into organizations and feel they truly are ready for promotion after only two months. Younger workers in prior generations have been ambitious and goal-oriented, but the fact that X'ers feel they deserve a particular job or type of work setting helps differentiate them from the rest of the pack. This obviously can be problematic and annoying for managers.

In fact, to some managers, this description of the X-workforce may sound repulsive and ludicrous. It may convince them even further that X'ers really are unappreciative whiners with no sense of reality nor regard for paying their dues. But for any positive change in the X-Crisis to occur, fulfilling the naked challenge requires an elemental acceptance — as difficult as it might be — of X'ers as a unique product of their values, expectations, perceptions of work, and the economic times in which they live. Otherwise gridlock, manifested in lower X'er productivity, loyalty, and morale, is assured.

The naked challenge for X'ers involves learning what their managers think is important, what irritates them and what they expect. It requires a clear understanding that managers are not there to baby-sit, and that they may be reluctant to bend over backwards and make concessions for the sake of satisfying X'ers. By gaining a deeper understanding of their managers' perspectives, members of the X-Generation will become more successful in getting their own workplace needs met.

THE NAKED MODEL EXPOSED

"All too often we are giving our young people cut flowers
when we should be teaching them to grow their own plants.
We are stuffing their heads with the products of earlier innovation
rather than teaching them to innovate.
We think of the mind as a storehouse to be filled
when we should be thinking of it as an instrument to be used."
John W. Gardner in *Self-Renewal*

Getting naked culminates with learning and utilizing the NAKED Model (see Figure 3), the principal tool of Naked Management. While the NAKED Model is simple, it is by no means arbitrary. Instead, it is purposeful, straightforward, and targeted. The five easy-to-remember dimensions are derived from X'er core values (see Figure 2) and directly address the issues of the X-Crisis. Each component represents an equally important learning element of Naked Management, yet none of them are designed to stand alone. The synthesis of these NAKED Model components creates powerful synergy and a management philosophy that is specifically matched to the needs of X'ers.

The interdependence of the NAKED components dictates that managers must embrace the entire model, not just one or two of the more salient points. For instance, actively involving X'ers in decision making (Active Involvement) loses its positive impact when they fail to receive credit (Key Recognition) for their good ideas. Along the same lines, managers who spell out exactly what they expect (Direct Communication) may be perceived by the X-workforce as condescending and authoritarian if they also incessantly micro-manage (hence, failing to provide Necessary Freedom). Going only part of the way with Naked Management is ultimately futile. Success in igniting and sustaining X-workforce motivation is contingent upon full-scale NAKED Model implementation.

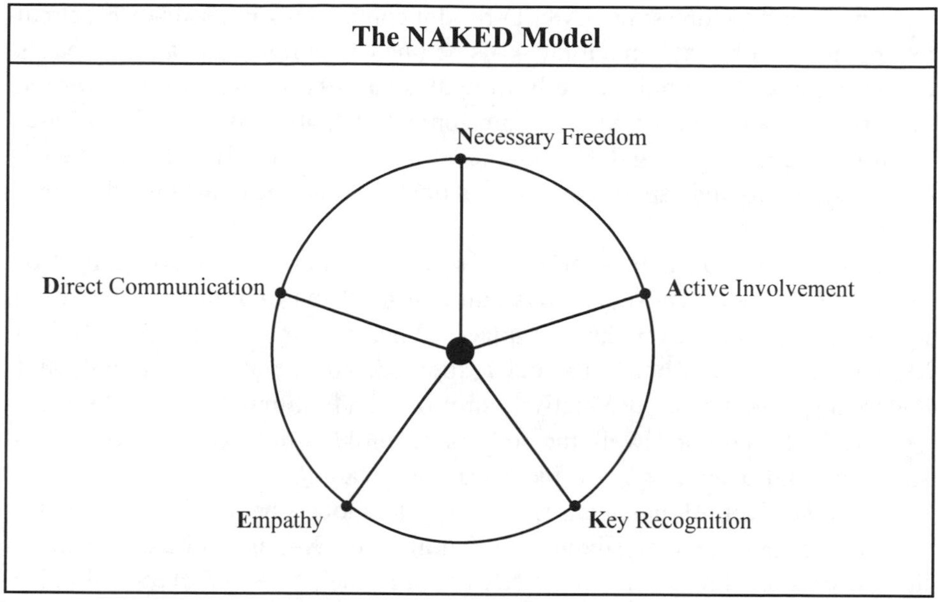

Figure 3

A NAKED FRAME OF MIND

"...If employees were to write a Bill of Rights, this is what it would contain:

- *Respect our thoughts, feelings, values, and fears.*
- *Respect our desire to lead and follow.*
- *Respect our unique strengths and differences.*
- *Respect our desire to participate and contribute.*
- *Respect our need to feel like a winner.*
- *Respect our desire to learn and develop.*
- *Respect our desire for a healthy workplace.*
- *Respect our personal and family life.*

...The bottom line...is showing people that you recognize and value their special worth as human beings."

Robert Rosen with Lisa Berger in
The Healthy Company: Eight Strategies to Develop People, Productivity, and Profits

Specifically addressing NAKED Model components in terms of practical examples and relevant behavioral skills begins with a final look at the process of getting naked. Attitude directly mitigates success in attaining the desired performance outcomes of Naked Management. Adopting the NAKED Model requires that managers and X'ers concentrate on the positive utility of each other's strengths and capabilities. Such a demeanor defines the "naked" frame of mind.

Having a naked frame of mind bears mutual benefits. Each component of the NAKED Model is designed to tap into those attributes of the X-Generation which are best suited for the workplace. When managers implement Naked Management, X'ers begin to feel respected, appreciated, included, and understood. Morale and productivity improve, and ultimately the bottom line gets met. Like a groundswell, the pent-up potential of the X-workforce surges and flows, unleashing new confidence and motivation.

However, not all managers find it easy to adopt a naked frame of mind. They may struggle with the thought of looking at the X-Generation in a positive light, especially if they truly believe X'ers fit the negative stereotypes of being lazy, bratty, ungrateful, presumptuous, and disloyal. In these instances, managers must also recognize that the onus for making forward progress is not entirely upon them. Naked Management, by design, is a two-way street. X'ers have as much of a role in implementing the NAKED Model as do their managers.

Therefore, it is imperative that X'ers too adopt a naked frame of mind. If members of the X-workforce are ever to form a partnership with managers, their attitudes must reflect an open willingness to work together. The more X'ers show a genuine appreciation for the experience and skills managers bring to the table — along with an understanding that their own expectations may at times be inflated or unrealistic — the greater the prospects for having their goodwill and acceptance reciprocated and their workplace needs fulfilled.

NAKED CHECKLIST: GETTING NAKED

Fulfillment of each of the following tasks is a key aspect of implementing Naked Management as it relates to this chapter. The listed items for managers and X'ers may be added to or revised to fit individual work environments or company policies.

For Managers:

_____ 1. ***Prepare for Naked Management through increased self-awareness.*** Identify what you expect from X'ers and address any self-imposed barriers, underlying resistance, or hidden agendas you may have.

_____ 2. ***Acknowledge and respect the ways in which X'ers differ from you.*** Be aware of what causes friction in your working relationship, paying careful attention to differences in values, expectations, and perceptions of work.

_____ 3. ***Learn the five points of the NAKED Model.*** Remember that these components are interdependent and must all be implemented for Naked Management to be truly effective.

_____ 4. ***Capitalize on X'ers' positive attributes.*** Focus on their strengths by adopting a naked frame of mind.

For X'ers:

_____ 1. ***Take responsibility for your experience in the workplace.*** Focus on what *you* do — or fail to do — that results in tension or conflict with your manager.

_____ 2. ***Know what your manager values.*** Understand what (s)he thinks is important and what (s)he expects.

_____ 3. ***Familiarize yourself with the NAKED Model.*** Your knowledge of these five components will help you define your own role in the Naked Management process.

_____ 4. ***Remember that Naked Management is a two-way street.*** Demonstrate an open willingness to work together with your manager by adopting a naked frame of mind. Show a genuine appreciation for the experience and skills (s)he brings to the table.

X'ERCISE 2: BARE ESSENTIALS

DIRECTIONS

The following questions are formatted for managers. **If you are an X'er, replace the word "X'ers" with "your manager" any time it appears in an item.** Write your answers in the spaces provided or on a separate sheet of paper. Then, discuss your answers with other managers and/or X'ers.

1. How do your values about work differ from those of X'ers? How are they the same?

2. What barriers cause friction between X'ers and you?

3. How willing are you to make changes in your working relationship with X'ers?

What will X'ers have to do to make implementing Naked Management worthwhile and/or tolerable?

4. Would you say your expectations of X'ers often are too high, too low, or just right?

Explain by giving a clear example.

5. What are some positive aspects of X'ers? How, if at all, do these attributes match what you are looking for in an employee?

NECESSARY FREEDOM

Top Ten Things Managers Do That Suffocate X'ers

10. Inundate them with instruction manuals and special tips on how to plug in their computers.
9. Only delegate tasks to them which are considered "safe" or "dummyproof."
8. Keep tabs on the exact moment they arrive at work and the second that they leave.
7. Put them in open cubicles within close enough range to monitor their phone conversations.
6. Cultivate hand-holding as the management style of choice.
5. Assume they can't walk and chew gum at the same time.
4. Give them mindless jobs at slave labor pay and expect them to feel challenged.
3. Watch over their shoulders to make sure they are doing things the "right" way.
2. Require that *all* their written communications — e.g., memos and thank you notes — get managerial approval.
1. Tell them they are empowered, yet treat them like incapable morons.

Corporate Office X'ers
Chicago, IL

IN X'ERS WE TRUST

"In the best workplaces, employees trust their managers, and the managers trust their employees.... Trust, in the workplace, simply means that employees are treated as partners and recognized as having something to contribute beyond brawn or manual dexterity or strong legs or arms."

Robert Levering and Milton Moskowitz
in *The 100 Best Companies to Work for in America*

X'ers need room to create and a chance to establish their own identity in the workplace. The notion of believing in the inherent abilities of members of the X-workforce and providing an environment conducive to their growth is encompassed in the first component of the NAKED model: Necessary Freedom. Implicitly, **Necessary Freedom means giving X'ers the autonomy, latitude, trust, and sense of entrepreneurialism they need to be productive and fulfilled.**

One of the most common ways managers violate this principle is by obsessively looking over X'ers' shoulders (often referred to as "checking" behavior). They want to know everything that happens, when it happens. They have tremendous difficulty letting go of the reigns for even a moment.Suspicion runs high with those who incessantly check. They are more than skeptical about granting X'ers the slightest degree of independence.

Because the X-workforce places great value on their ability to think for themselves, they interpret checking and constant over-supervision as a symbolic lack of managerial confidence in their wherewithal to get the job done:

"My boss must think I'm a blithering idiot. Every day he tells me to make sure I greet the customers. He reminds me like clockwork. After the second or third time, you can imagine that I've got the message. I'm quite capable of performing my job without him breathing down my neck all the time."

Pam, 20 — video store sales associate in Bloomington, IN

X'ers want the authority to make basic decisions without always having to get approval. They seek task ownership, as opposed to being spoon-fed. They crave to do their work the way that they honestly feel will result in the highest quality product, regardless of how things were done in the past.In a major way, they need to know that they are unconditionally trusted and have been given the authority to do what seems right in the situations they daily encounter. They want managers to treat them like capable adults. This means giving X'ers the freedom to evaluate choices and make on-the-job decisions, which are major tenants of empowerment and total quality theory.

Yet, many managers find it difficult to put decision-making power in the uncalloused hands of the X-Generation. Several suggestions for overcoming this barrier consist of spending sufficient time on training, starting X'ers on smaller projects and easing them into bigger ones, providing X'ers with mentors, establishing ground rules and reasonable limitations that govern the provision of Necessary Freedom and setting realistic expectations that things may not run smoothly at first.

In exchange for expanded autonomy, X'ers must indicate to managers the degree of independence which best suits them. For instance, those members of the X-workforce who prefer a great deal of latitude can inform their supervisors that they would like to work on projects which permit them to use their creativity to solve problems. The more information managers have, the better equipped they are to gauge X'ers' individual need levels for Necessary Freedom.

NAKED SUCCESS: PROFILE OF A **LEVY RESTAURANTS** X'ER

Company: **THE LEVY RESTAURANTS**
Industry: Restaurant and Specialty Concessions
Headquarters: Chicago, Illinois

Key Facts: Since it's founding in 1978, The Levy Restaurants has grown from a single delicatessen in Chicago to a renowned industry leader. Currently, it operates an impressive list of over 40 restaurants, sports, and entertainment venues, and off-site and major event catering in 10 national markets. Award-winning restaurants include Chicago's Spiaggia, Bistro 110, and the Blackhawk Lodge; Portobello Yacht Club at Walt Disney World® in Orlando; and Charlotte's Bistro 100. Sports and Entertainment Group operations boast landmark venues such as Chicago's Wrigley Field, Comiskey Park, Arlington International Racecourse, and McCormick Place; St. Louis' Kiel Center and America's Center, Kansas City's Arrowhead Stadium, and Portland's Rose Garden Arena. Most recently, the company teamed up with Steven Spielberg and Jeffrey Katzenberg to own and manage DIVE!, an innovative "underwater" restaurant concept featuring gourmet submarine sandwiches. DIVE! broke ground in Los Angeles in 1994, Las Vegas in 1995, and Barcelona in 1996, with plans to open soon in many more major cities.

> *"I feel valued and trusted here — my boss shares the big picture with me and gives me the ball on major projects."*

Name: Alison
Title: Marketing Director
Age: 29

Tenure/History: At age 21, Alison started working as an intern at a leading national department store in Boston. After being promoted to regional public relations director in Chicago, her supervisor of four years, Carol, left for a new job as vice president of marketing for The Levy Restaurants. She quickly recruited Alison, then 26, as public relations director and marketing manager of The Levy Restaurants. Alison was promoted within a year to senior marketing manager and then marketing director the following year.She currently is on the fast track to upper management.

Motivating Things About Her Job: *"My boss can't be involved in the day-to-day of my job. When we need to do marketing research for a new venture, the type of directive I get from her is, 'Go in and figure it out, create an action plan, then fill me in.' I have her complete trust to use my best judgment. Most of the time, I wind up teaching her. It creates an interdependency. It's great — and very rewarding!"*

Motivating Things About Her Boss: *"Carol knows that I don't need a lot of direction. She feels perfectly comfortable saying, 'Here's the event. Here's the goal. Go for it.' It's almost intuitive, the relationship we have. She doesn't micro-manage me. I guess that's why I've stuck with her for six years. I couldn't imagine working for anyone else."*

What Keeps Her From Leaving: *"Carol puts me on a long rope, and every once in awhile I almost hang myself. But that's okay here; it's learning. It's all part of it. I'm allowed — and encouraged — to add my own touch to my work. Decisions aren't made for me. I certainly learn more from my own bad decisions than getting reprimanded for someone else's."*

Most Memorable "Naked Moment": *"By Carol giving me so much freedom, I was able to create the marketing model we now use to build all of our Sports and Entertainment Group businesses. Carol gave me the space I needed, and I figured the whole thing out. It's so incredible when your boss empowers you like that."*

A LONG, LONG ROPE

"When I have been able to transform a group...into a community of <u>*learners*</u>, *then the excitement has been almost beyond belief. To free curiosity; to permit individuals to go charging off in new directions dictated by their own interests; to unleash the sense of inquiry; to open everything to questioning and exploration; to recognize that everything is in a process of change — here is an experience I can never forget....Out of such a context arise...the kind of individuals who can live in a delicate but ever-changing balance between what is presently known and the flowing, moving, altering, problems and facts of the future."*

Carl Rogers in *Freedom to Learn*

A key aspect of Necessary Freedom deals with giving X'ers a feeling of control over their working environment. Although juxtaposing the terms "freedom" and "control" may seem contradictory, the former actually paves the way for the latter in the case of the X-workforce. It is the absence of rigid constraints and entangled bureaucracy that provides X'ers with a sense of comfort and security. In other words, X'ers like it when managers are not constantly *telling* them what to do.

The role of the manager in the eyes of the X-Generation is someone with whom they can share ideas, troubleshoot anticipated or recurring problems, and ask for help at any time. A boss is the objective consultant, the person who can assist them, train them, mentor them, and refocus them. They want this overseeing individual to let them essentially run their own show. The implied challenge for managers is to provide X'ers with a long enough rope without choking on the fear that they will hang themselves.

Recognizing that the X-workforce thrives on autonomy stands out as a significant motivating factor of which managers can take advantage. By promoting an organizational culture of freedom, managers can effectively foster X'ers' interdependence, tap their creative juices, grow their self-confidence, and enhance their work productivity. A climate of "intra-entrepreneurialism" — true Necessary Freedom — forces X'ers to embrace change and excel amidst the dynamic demands of the competitive workplace.

An example of Necessary Freedom in action can be found in the distribution of tasks or projects. Usually managers say to X'ers, *"Here is what I want you to do, and this is how I want you to do it."* They falsely assume that they have provided that individual with autonomy because the task has been delegated.

An alternative way of giving the same directive would be: *"As you know, this is one of our performance goals. I'd like you to come up with a plan for achieving this objective while staying within the annual budget. I'll be happy to provide you with any resources you need to get the job done."* These statements focus on a specific bottom-line outcome while giving Necessary Freedom to X'ers — *full* task ownership and discretion about how the job gets done.

But to make Necessary Freedom plausible, X'ers must earn their managers' respect, demonstrate they can be trusted, and show they can handle autonomy. They have to take the initiative to ask questions instead of allowing problems to build and fester. Members of the X-Generation also need to convey their appreciation when they are given control and decision-making power.The X'er-manager relationship has to be firmly grounded in reciprocal respect and commitment.

NAKED SUCCESS: PROFILE OF A **HOME DEPOT** X'ER

Company: **THE HOME DEPOT**
Industry: Home Center Retailer
Headquarters: Atlanta, Georgia

Key Facts: The Home Depot was founded in 1978, and is now North America's largest home center retailer. The company employs about 80,000 people and operates more than 400 warehouse-style home centers in 31 states plus 20 stores in three Canadian provinces. Gross annual sales exceed $12 billion. The Home Depot expects to be operating more than 850 stores by the end of fiscal 1998. Each store stocks approximately 40,000 to 50,000 different kinds of building materials, home improvement supplies, and lawn and garden products and offers free in-store consultation from professional designers.Special credits go to The Home Depot's unprecedented level of customer service among warehouse-style retailers and its progressive corporate culture which includes Team Depot. Team Depot is an organized volunteer force developed to promote volunteer activities within the local communities the stores serve.

"I can't even think of why I wouldn't still be working here in 15 years."

Name: Joe
Title: Department Supervisor — Kitchen, Cabinets and Plumbing
Age: 28

Tenure/History: Joe started working part-time for The Home Depot in floor sales at age 22. Once he saw how much growth potential there was, he quit his other job and invested his full energy into The Home Depot. At 25, he was promoted to supervisor of the kitchen and counters department.One year later he was put in charge of the electrical department, a significant increase in responsibility. By age 28, he was promoted to his current position where he is in charge of the largest revenue-producing department in the store — more than 80% of all retail sales — worth close to $8 million a year.

Motivating Things About His Job: *"It's like being an entrepreneur where I run my own store within a larger store. What I mean is that I have a sense of ownership. I am valued for my abilities. There's no hand-holding — the company wants me to think for myself. It makes me proud to call this store 'my store,' too."*

Motivating Things About His Boss: *"Dan, the store manager, takes the time to come out on the floor every day, and consistently with a positive attitude. He greets you and helps you feel good about yourself. Because he knows his stuff, he makes sure you know yours, too, by walking with you down the aisles and pointing things out. Instead of bandaging problems, he teaches you to cure them. He sets a great example. I want to be like that."*

What Keeps Him From Leaving: *"I can go out and do anything that I think needs to be done to make this department run better. I have total control over what I do. If I make a mistake, I'll go and work on it until I get it right. In addition to the money, that's what drives me. My career will happen here at The Home Depot — there is not a doubt in my mind."*

Most Memorable "Naked Moment": *"Every promotion I have received at The Home Depot has been my most memorable experience. To me, it is a sign that I have come a long way."*

NO ROOM TO SNEEZE

"Proxemics is the study of how we use space and what that use says about us. It is based on the concept that people, like animals, are territorial beings and will protect 'their space.' At work, people exhibit this territorial behavior in regard to their offices, their possessions, and even their ideas....Thus, supervisors should be aware of the dynamics of personal space and respect employees' space in order to promote comfortable relationships."

Jane Whitney Gibson in
The Supervisory Challenge: Principles and Practices

In the scope of Necessary Freedom, personal space represents another concern for managers and X'ers. Cost-conscious times prohibit giving every new hire a huge office with elaborate mahogany furniture and a window view. With great frequency in corporate settings, freshly recruited X'ers find themselves sharing desks in cramped cubicles. Privacy is scarce in these confined quarters. X'ers who work in non-office environments (e.g., supermarkets, restaurants, hotels, banks, factories, department stores, retail shops) also find it difficult to get a break from the action. Taking time for themselves may not be an option during peak periods of operation.

Managers, too, may feel this personal space squeeze. In addition to a regular workload, their direct interface with X'ers can be continual. Some managers simply close their office doors and program their phones to "send all calls." A more productive method geared toward longer-term results, however, consists of identifying and planning mental hygiene "release time" for both X'ers and themselves. Examples include making lunch breaks mandatory (since no one ever has time for them), utilizing compensation time for extra hours worked, permitting brief personal phone calls if they do not interfere with satisfying customers or meeting business deadlines, providing opportunities to participate in stress or time management classes, and trying to generally be less intrusive. Since these suggestions may not be applicable to every job context, managers need to put the onus upon themselves to identify those interventions that are most appropriate for their particular workplace.

X'ers, on the other hand, need to make managers aware of the ways in which their personal space gets violated. They must also propose remedies which would alleviate or eliminate these matters. For instance, it is *their* responsibility to tell managers that going to lunch is an important aspect of their day that they rarely get to enjoy. Only by speaking up and making practical recommendations will X'ers be able to gain the breathing room they desire.

MUTUAL BENEFITS

*"Why Is It
That Some Managers
Are Typically
Running Out Of Time
While Their Staffs
Are Typically
Running Out Of Work?*

Ken Blanchard, Bill Oncken, Jr. and Hal Burrows in *The One Minute Manager Meets the Monkey*

Members of the X-Generation welcome the implementation of Necessary Freedom in the workplace. Being trusted, having a sense of intra-entrepreneurialism and getting enough personal space are key growth conditions that most X'ers pine to experience. They thirst to be respected for their innate potential and ingenuity. Necessary Freedom helps kindle the flame of self-reliance for the X-workforce while reinforcing the fact that their relationship with managers can be positive and productive. This results in a rise in job enthusiasm, increased company loyalty, and an inner motivation to work harder.

Necessary Freedom also pays additional dividends to managers. One highlight of these benefits is time. Since time is scarce, any tool that augments it becomes infinitely desirable. When managers provide X'ers with autonomy and a sense of control, it frees them up to do other things. They become liberated instead of being bound by the compulsion to micro-manage and check. Letting the X-workforce have additional space only means that managers gain quality time and breathing room of their own.

Another reason for managers to apply Necessary Freedom techniques with the X-workforce is earn their trust and respect. This translates into positive, performance-linked results. For instance, when provided with the autonomy to solve problems on their own, X'ers may find more efficient or effective ways to perform tasks or think of solutions which no one else had previously considered. They truly begin to care about the best interests of the company in addition to their own individual welfare. Once X'ers feel valued, a certain pride in workmanship and animated team spirit develop. By issuing them greater responsibilities and more personal space — and through the facilitation of an intra-entrepreneurial working environment — managers send a clear message to X'ers that they believe in them and the potential they have to do great things.

NAKED CHECKLIST: NECESSARY FREEDOM

Fulfillment of each of the following tasks is a key aspect of implementing Naked Management as it relates to this chapter. The listed items for managers and X'ers may be added to or revised to fit individual work environments or company policies.

For Managers:

___1. ***Don't be a "checker"—X'ers want to know that you trust them.*** Avoid looking over their shoulders. Issue them expanded autonomy so they will feel empowered. Let them think for themselves, use their best judgment, and make basic decisions without having to get managerial approval each time.

___2. ***Find your comfort zone with Necessary Freedom.*** Set realistic expectations, start off slow, and provide sufficient mentorship and training. Establish guidelines which ensure the degree of control you want to retain.

___3. ***Acknowledge X'ers personal space needs as well as your own.*** Plan mental hygiene "release" time (e.g., mandatory lunches, stress management classes), allow for compensation time and try to be less intrusive.

___4. ***Foster an organizational climate of intra-entrepreneurialism.*** Truly give X'ers the ball and let them run with it. Grant them task ownership and discretion over task execution within the scope of bottom-line objectives.

For X'ers:

___1. ***Let managers know if they are becoming "checkers" or control freaks.*** Identify the precise behavior and explain how it makes you feel.

___2. ***Indicate to managers how much independence you prefer.*** Be specific about the context of this envisioned autonomy, your desire for creative problem-solving opportunities, and whether or not you wish to be in a project leadership position.

___3. ***Make managers aware of personal space violations.*** Openly discuss infringements on your privacy and propose plausible remedies. Take responsibility for speaking up and getting the breathing room you need.

___4. ***Demonstrate to your manager that you can be trusted with complete autonomy.*** Regularly review your progress and performance, and take the initiative to ask questions instead of allowing problems to build and fester. Also, convey your appreciation for being given a great deal of control and decision-making power.

X'ERCISE 3: IN THE NAME OF FREEDOM

DIRECTIONS

The following items are designed to help you assess your strategy for putting the NAKED Model component "Necessary Freedom" into practice. Write your answers in the spaces provided or on a separate sheet of paper. Then, discuss your responses with other managers and/or X'ers.

1a. **(for managers only):**
How much freedom would your X'ers say you currently give them?
   a. a lot
   b. a little
   c. none at all

1b. **(for X'ers only):**
How much freedom does your manager currently give you?
   a. a lot
   b. a little
   c. none at all

2. List three potential benefits and risks associated with giving X'ers more freedom:

Benefits

1. ______________________________

2. ______________________________

3. ______________________________

Risks

1. ____________________

2. ____________________

3. ____________________

3. What are three ways to minimize the risks you listed in Question 2?

   1. ____________________

   2. ____________________

   3. ____________________

4. Name five things a manager can do to provide Necessary Freedom for X'ers (include ideas that address the issues of trust, personal space, and intra-entrepreneurialism):

   1. ____________________

   2. ____________________

   3. ____________________

   4. ____________________

   5. ____________________

4

ACTIVE INVOLVEMENT

TOP TEN USES FOR AN X'ER SUGGESTION BOX

10. Ballot box for "Slacker of the Year."
9. Great place to hide something you don't want anyone else to read.
8. Firewood for management "outdoor adventure" retreat.
7. Reminder that X'ers really do have a bone to pick.
6. Endless source of scratch paper.
5. Written forum for X'ers to whine.
4. Manager reality check: X'ers are here to stay.
3. Guaranteed collector's item.
2. Token marketing perk to lure unknowing X'er job applicants.
1. Extra trash can — where do you think these suggestions get dumped anyway?

Disillusioned X'ers
Newark, NJ

WHEN I WANT YOUR OPINION I'LL GIVE IT TO YOU

"[Baby] Boomer managers claim to be seeking younger employees' input when in reality they couldn't care less what Xers think.... What really grates on Xers is when bosses publicly avow participatory management but then cling to their old hierarchical ways. ...THE BOTTOM LINE with twentysomethings is that they'll respond if boomer managers put meaning into the buzzwords they're prone to mouthing..."

Suneel Ratan's *Fortune* article:
"Why Busters Hate Boomers"

Almost every person who has worked can name a boss or secondary supervisor they know who personifies the 1950s-style manager motif of *"just shut up and do your job because we didn't hire you to think, speak, or ask questions."* Ironically, in an era where total quality management and internal customer service programs dominate the training agendas and public image campaigns of most companies, traditional images of line-staff hierarchies proliferate at every level. The antiquated notion that employees are "worker bees" is still more than tacitly implied for the X-Generation.

One manager volunteered the following insights into the quandary over why things are slow to change:

"The problem is that young employees feel helpless. They want to put their two cents in and affect decisions. But the reality is that if they want to survive here, they need to have a soldier mentality. This means march when they are told and follow the plan to precise specifications. We have a business to run."

Janet, 37 — flight manager for major
airline (on layover in Houston, TX)

An overwhelming feeling of being unable to take an active role in matters which directly affect them disheartens growing numbers of X'ers, as illustrated in the words of a despondent twenty-something from the San Francisco Bay area:

"Assignments are just given to me. My opinions are looked at as secondary to what my boss thinks. As you might imagine, I have been aggressively submitting my résumé to companies — many of them, our competitors — which still seem to care about keeping their people involved in the process, regardless of their age, job title, or experience."

Andy, 23 — programmer, software development company in Palo Alto, CA

Active Involvement, the second point of the NAKED Model, emphasizes the need for managers to make X'ers full partners in the quest to succeed and win in a competitive, if not cutthroat, marketplace. X'ers like to question policies and procedures that seem ambiguous, unclear, or outdated. To some managers, this sounds like whining. Yet the undeniable fact is that the X-workforce wants to be involved in what ultimately affects them, regardless of how their behavior is interpreted. They are interested in improving the way work is distributed, managed, and evaluated. They see themselves having a voice in identifying team objectives and in finding solutions to work problems.

When managers implement Active Involvement, members of the X-Generation gain a say in the action, a stake in outcomes, and the means to stay involved in strategic issues. Combining this key NAKED Model component with Necessary Freedom establishes a broader base for empowering, engaging, and motivating X'ers. In turn, this pays off in better X-workforce performance and stability.

A SAY IN THE ACTION

"...if employee motivational levels — and consequently performance — are to be increased, it becomes especially important to involve the employees themselves in a cooperative venture aimed at improving output, for after all they too have a stake in what happens to the organization. Thus, one key factor in motivating employees is to engage them more fully in the processes aimed at attaining organizational effectiveness. Without employee cooperation and support, a great deal of managerial energy can be wasted."

Richard Steers and Lyman Porter in *Motivation and Work Behavior*

A popular intervention for collecting X'er input involves the creation of an employee suggestion program. While the various methodologies for accomplishing this project differ in degree of cost and sophistication, the common assumption and guiding intention is that X'ers will gain a direct line into the boardroom. Their fresh ideas and cost-saving tips as well as grievances are routed to management in hopes of improving current conditions.

Unfortunately, the reality in many companies is that suggestions frequently get tossed or totally ignored. For this brand of Active Involvement to be effective, *each* submission needs to be examined and considered. Equally important is that a viable and maintainable system for implementing meritable ideas must be put in place. It is imperative that X'ers get timely responses to their proposals and notifications of suggestions which result in operational modifications or improvements.

Related to the concept of suggestion systems, managers can provide opportunities for members of the X-Generation to participate in the evaluation of selected proposals. Letting X'ers do research and cost-benefit studies on their own ideas encompasses the essence of Active Involvement. They take instant pride in being able to submit their efficiency and effectiveness assessments to the appropriate reviewing parties. Especially in cases where submissions gain approval, managers have the opportunity to boost X'er morale and feelings of ownership to the highest level by placing them in charge of materializing a feasible action plan for executing their ideas.

If managers conscientiously make Active Involvement a staple of suggestion systems, X'ers must make it their mission to employ tactful persistence when following up on their submissions. Not only may the use of etiquette result in getting a more prompt response, it can change managers' perceptions of them from "impatient and insolent" to "ambitious and forthright." Members of the X-workforce can additionally take the onus upon themselves to prepare cost-benefit analyses for inclusion with their submitted suggestions. Consequently, the potential benefits and savings associated with these proposals are more apt to appear well thought-out and potentially viable.

NAKED SUCCESS: PROFILE OF A **RITZ-CARLTON** X'ER

Company: **THE RITZ-CARLTON**, NAPLES (Florida)
Industry: Luxury Hotel and Resort
Headquarters: Atlanta, Georgia

Key Facts: The Ritz-Carlton, Naples, which opened in 1985, was the first resort property conceived by The Ritz-Carlton Hotel Company, now hailed as the world's finest luxury hotel company and winner of the Malcolm Baldridge National Quality Award for 1992. The resort's 463 guest rooms, including 28 suites, underwent a multimillion dollar refurbishment in preparation for the property's 10th anniversary. The comfortable accommodations offer balconies with views of the Gulf of Mexico. Rooms are furnished with painted Louis IV-style furniture and marbled baths. The hotel itself evokes grandeur with a classic, symmetrical U-shape, arches, courtyards, stone fountains, and manicured gardens. The design gives guests unexpected vistas at every turn. Even the fitness center offers exercisers lovely views of the rose garden through French doors. During the December through April season, afternoon tea is served in the lobby lounge. The acclaimed Ritz-Carlton customer service abounds, perhaps most notably as valets greet guests by name whether they pick up their car in an hour or after eight days.

> *"You're treated like an equal here. Your participation and involvement are expected, not questioned."*

Name: Mark
Title: Rooms Executive
Age: 28

Tenure/History: With his father working in the hospitality industry for decades, Mark remembers spending most of his childhood growing up in and around hotels. Mark came aboard at The Ritz-Carlton, Naples, as the assistant director of housekeeping when he was 25 years old. Within three months, he was promoted to director of housekeeping. Only two years later, Mark became the assistant director of rooms at this five-star, five-diamond luxury resort. As an addendum to this success profile, Mark was recently promoted to the position of rooms executive at The Ritz-Carlton, Kansas City.

Motivating Things About His Job: *"I like being involved in group decisions. In my job here, I'm viewed as the expert. When we do internal defect reports, I have a say. There is also a 'good idea board' which empowers you to make things happen. It truly means you have the ball and can get people together or talk directly to corporate — regardless of what your job is. There is a definite feeling at the Ritz that it's okay to say 'we can do it differently.'"*

Motivating Things About His Boss: *"Alexandra, my boss, is both people- and task-focused. She is personable, funny, and loves to joke around. Although she is very direct, she has tremendous interpersonal skills. Because she holds you accountable for your work, one thing is for sure: you know what you are supposed to be doing."*

What Keeps Him From Leaving: *"You are valued here. The Ritz-Carlton credo, 'We are ladies and gentlemen serving ladies and gentlemen' is an ingrained and mandated part of the culture here. It promotes a positive perception of people, which reflects back on how we feel about management. The 'I care' mentality is like the gift that keeps on giving."*

Most Memorable "Naked Moment": *"I was really pushing for a mandatory five-day work week. My boss soon put me in charge of forming a task force to look into it. I got a group of eight managers together from around the country. We met twice in Atlanta, and in the end, figured the whole thing out without payroll costs increasing. I feel thrilled to have been in on the ground floor."*

BEYOND THE SUGGESTION BOX

"As work becomes more multi-dimensional, it also becomes more substantive ...work becomes more satisfying, since workers achieve a greater sense of completion, closure, and accomplishment from their jobs. They actually perform a whole job — a process or a subprocess — that by definition produces a result that somebody cares about. Process performers share many of the challenges and rewards of entrepreneurs. They are focused on customers whose satisfaction is their aim. They're not just trying to keep the boss happy or to work through the bureaucracy."

Michael Hammer and James Champy in
Reengineering the Corporation: A Manifesto for Business Revolution

Active Involvement of the X-workforce can be achieved through other means than employee suggestion systems alone. Innate in the hearts of X'ers is the keen desire to be a part of something bigger — something greater — whether on the job or outside work. X'ers yearn to contribute to a larger whole and to feel a meaningful connection to that entity. X'ers want to grow and evolve by fully participating in those things that directly impact their future, free time, and overall quality of life. In the sphere of the workplace, they long to experience collective synergy with their managers and co-workers.

Essentially, the X-workforce wants an element of control. They hunger for an integral role in decision making that goes beyond just submitting their professional input and creative thoughts into a wooden suggestion box. Readily, they await the chance to step in and hit the ground running. Here again, X'ers may be perceived as impetuous, too big for their boots, or simply unrealistic. If the goal is win-win, then the key for managers is to provide avenues for Active Involvement which will ingrain members of the X-Generation in the very fabric of their organizations, thus setting the stage for progress. Bill Byham depicts this idea in his renowned book *Zapp! The Lightning of Empowerment*:

When you have been Zapped, you feel like...
Your job belongs to you.
You are responsible.
Your job counts for something.
You know where you stand.
You have some say in how things are done.
Your job is a part of who you are.
You have some control over your work.

Following are several strategies that managers can use to "Zapp" X'ers. Each of them stem from variations on the theme of total quality and universally stress the importance of giving X'ers a stake in analyzing, designing, and shaping business processes. Beginning with performance objectives, managers need to involve the X-workforce in setting short-term and long-term performance objectives. Part of this process includes showing X'ers the "big picture." The introduction of this broader scope aids members of the X-Generation in comprehending the relative significance of their jobs and subsequently enriches their sense of purpose. For this reason, many managers have recently begun showing their employees financial profit and loss statements, a practice sometimes referred to as "open book" management.

In the highly acclaimed Leadership is an Art, Max DePree discusses the following with regard to the importance of managers sharing critical information with their staffs:

> *...We must understand that access to pertinent information is essential to getting a job done. The right to know is basic. Moreover, it is better to err on the side of sharing too much information than risk leaving someone in the dark. Information is power, but it is pointless power if hoarded. Power must be shared for an organization or a relationship to work.*

Furthermore, managers can provide Active Involvement for X'ers by putting them on project teams, strategic planning committees, or special task forces. They can also introduce X'ers to influential people in the organization as well as valued clients or customers with whom they can build productive relationships. Trade groups, community service councils, and networking consortiums are other outlets in which X'ers may readily participate.

X'ers have to assume a forefront position in helping to facilitate Active Involvement. They must take the initiative to identify interdepartmental teams, task forces, or ad hoc committees that interest them along with trade associations they wish to join. They need to inquire about salary structures, annual performance goals, or anything else which will paint a more lucid picture of their job mobility and potential career track in the company. Finally, Active Involvement entails X'ers asking their managers for direct participation in total quality initiatives and in the reengineering of job-relevant business processes and systems.

NAKED SUCCESS: PROFILE OF A **PEPSICO** X'ER

Company: **PEPSICO, INC.**
Industry: Consumer Products
Headquarters: Purchase, New York

Key Facts: PepsiCo, Inc. is among the most successful consumer products companies in the world, with annual revenues of $25 billion and about 423,000 employees. Some of PepsiCo's brand names are nearly 100 years old, but the corporation is relatively young. PepsiCo, Inc. was founded in 1965 through the merger of Pepsi-Cola Company and Frito-Lay, Inc. PepsiCo divisions operate in three major businesses: beverages, snack foods, and restaurants. PepsiCo has achieved a leadership position in each of these business segments. The corporation's beverage division, Pepsi-Cola North America, alone generates $8 billion. PepsiCo's brand names and restaurants are some of the best known and most respected in the world, and include: Pepsi, Diet Pepsi, Slice, Mountain Dew, and Mug brand soft drinks; Lipton teas (a joint venture); Ocean Spray juices (distribution only); Taco Bell, Pizza Hut, KFC, Chevys, California Pizza Kitchen, and Hot 'n Now restaurants; Frito Lay, Ruffles, Lay's, Doritos, Cheetos, Tostitos, Santitas, Rold Gold, Hostess, and SunChips brand snack foods.

"If you have the skills to make it happen, this is one place that gives you a chance."

Name: Julie
Title: Human Resources Director
Age: 29

Tenure/History: Upon graduating college in 1988, Julie was recruited by PepsiCo. At age 22, she started out as an employee relations representative in California, and was soon transferred to Phoenix, where she was promoted to senior employee relations representative. By 24, she was back in California as a human resources manager, and a year later her job doubled in responsibilities as HR manager for 600 employees. At 27, Julie was promoted to the corporate office to negotiate labor contracts. Next, after working on a special project in San Diego, she returned to New York to specialize in compensation. Now, at

29, Julie is in Michigan, where she is an HR director responsible for 2,000 people.

Motivating Things About Her Job: *"I really like change. What has been great about my seven years with PepsiCo is the job rotation, diversity of geographic settings and continual expansion of job breadth. It forces me to learn — all of the different experiences, different markets, and different co-workers. Early in your career, it's easy to be flexible. You can broaden yourself by accepting opportunities that come your way, which is more difficult to do later on when you might have family or other commitments."*

Motivating Things About Her Bosses: *"All of my supervisors at PepsiCo have given me tremendous opportunities to grow. They allow me to demonstrate what I can contribute by putting me in "stretch" positions that force me to grow and be challenged. They want you to become well-rounded and learn new skills."*

What Keeps Her From Leaving: *"What keeps me here is the continual challenge of the job and the sense of accomplishment it brings. The PepsiCo team has given me a lot of support and opportunities for advancement."*

Most Memorable "Naked Moment": *"My latest assignment is great because it is truly the culmination of all the learning experiences I have had with PepsiCo — hands-on in the field and strategic/big picture at corporate. I am on a business unit team where I am able to see the fruits of my labors. It's very satisfying to see your efforts pay off in a way that makes the business grow."*

BORED, NOT LAZY

> *"...Twentysomethings have tremendous capacity to process lots of information... The theory is that while Xers may have a limited attention span, they are able to concentrate that attention on multiple sources of information."*
>
> *Training's* Bob Filipczak in *"It's Just a Job: Generation X at Work"*

Some managers will always contend that the X-workforce is laden with lazy slackers. It may surprise them to know, however, that many X'ers are tremendously bored. A significant facet of Active Involvement deals with creating a challenging work environment for the X-Generation. X'ers are hungry to learn and grow. They yearn to be stretched and pushed. They want to be placed in situations which demand perseverance and require their personal attention. X'ers *will* rise to the occasion if given the chance. The trick is for managers to tap into their well of potential via stimulating tasks and assignments which provide Active Involvement.

Some extremely effective ways to pique X'ers' interest include the following: enlarging the breadth and depth of their jobs, having them prepare for and present at important meetings, setting high but attainable goals, offering performance-based training so that they can develop new and marketable skills, asking them what types of projects excite them (and how *they* would propose integrating these activities into their job descriptions), exposing them to different parts of the company's total operations through job rotation, introducing the latest technology to them and letting them use it, staying well-informed on the latest trends and industry developments (X'ers hold tremendous respect for supervisors who know their stuff), and encouraging them to design their own work execution plans.

Managers need X'ers' assistance, though, to accomplish the goal of creating challenge through Active Involvement. The only realistic way for them to know how enticing and demanding a task appears to the X-workforce is for X'ers to tell them. This input, if not requested by managers, must come unsolicited from X'ers. Other information that X'ers need to indicate includes personal work interests, areas of expertise, skill deficiencies, future career plans, and priorities. Consequently, managers will be able to pinpoint job duties which intrinsically challenge and thus motivate the X-Generation.

Having fun at work also helps break job monotony for X'ers. They thrive in companies which recognize fun as a necessary tenant of the organizational climate. X'ers relate well to bosses who know how to offset rigid bureaucracy with a good sense of humor. At the gut level, they cherish employment in a company where happiness is not only permitted, it is encouraged.

When it comes to promoting levity in the workplace with X'ers, managers have a limitless set of options that incorporate the concept of Active Involvement. Casual days or dress-down Fridays are just one spin. The X-workforce especially likes after-work happy hours, off-site meetings, pot-luck dinners, and celebrating positive achievements (as well as birthdays). Ultimately, a combination of these types of activities is apt to improve morale and provide productive energy for managers and X'ers alike, as long as ethical guidelines, professionalism, and basic reason prevail amidst the fun.

Overall, the return on utilizing Active Involvement with the X-Generation is that they become stakeholders, which elicits feelings of connectedness and self-worth. This engenders X-workforce commitment and team spirit. As a result, X'ers take pride in meeting deadlines, fulfilling performance objectives, and curtailing behaviors which might otherwise aggravate or provoke their managers.

NAKED CHECKLIST: ACTIVE INVOLVEMENT

Fulfillment of each of the following tasks is a key aspect of implementing Naked Management as it relates to this chapter. The listed items for managers and X'ers may be added to or revised to fit individual work environments or company policies.

For Managers:

___ 1. ***Make X'ers full partners by actively involving them in the quest to succeed and win.*** Refrain from using an autocratic style to get results. Keep in mind that members of the X-workforce are real people, not worker bees.

___ 2. ***Allocate sufficient time and human resources toward managing suggestion systems.*** Make sure *each* entry gets examined and considered. The system needs to be viable and maintainable so that X'ers get prompt notification regarding the status of their submitted input.

___ 3. ***Provide opportunities for the X-Generation to evaluate their own ideas.*** Give them the approval to do cost-benefit studies and let them present their proposals to the appropriate reviewing parties. Place them in charge of materializing an execution plan for accepted submissions.

___ 4. ***Give X'ers a stake in analyzing, designing and shaping business processes which ultimately affect them.*** Include them while setting short and long term goals. Enlist them in projects from start to finish so that they are exposed to "the big picture." Consider sharing departmental profit and loss statements, then train them to interpret these data.

___ 5. ***Designate X'ers as members of project teams and encourage them to join professional groups outside of work.*** Select them for cross-functional task forces, strategic planning groups, and ad hoc committees. Inform them of trade associations, networking consortiums, and community services in which they may wish to participate.

___ 6. ***Create a challenging work environment for X'ers and make fun and laughter a priority.*** Enlarge the scope of their positions, invite them to present at big meetings, rotate their jobs, and focus on their individual interests. Also, institute casual days, form softball teams, do festive pot-luck dinners, hold off-site meetings, celebrate positive achievements and, most of all, maintain a good sense of humor.

For X'ers:

__ 1. ***Make it your mission to follow up on suggestions you submit to management.*** Be tactful but persistent if the system stalls. Take the onus upon yourself to prepare cost-benefit analyses of your ideas, then submit them to your manager.

__ 2. ***Help facilitate the process of Active Involvement.*** Take the initiative to identify internal teams and professional groups outside of work that you have an interest in joining. Ask your manager for direct representation in decisions and discussions regarding job-relevant business processes.

__ 3. ***Get "the big picture."*** Inquire about salary structures, long-term performance goals and anything else which will elucidate your current job mobility or career path with the company. Understand the significance of your position in relation to the rest of the organization.

__ 4. ***Give input to managers on how they can successfully challenge you.*** Tell them how difficult or easy tasks are. Express your personal work interests, areas of expertise, and career plans for the future so that managers can identify the best ways to motivate you.

__ 5. ***Use common sense while having fun in the workplace.*** Adhere to ethical and professional guidelines. Take care that practical jokes and your sense of humor do not personally offend anyone, damage property, or become excessive. Remember that a good laugh is no excuse for slacking off.

X'ERCISE 4: THE POWER OF SUGGESTION

DIRECTIONS

The following items are designed to help you assess your strategy for putting the NAKED Model component "**A**ctive Involvement" into practice. Write your answers in the spaces provided or on a separate sheet of paper. Then, discuss your responses with other managers and/or X'ers.

1a. **(for managers only):**
How good of a job would your X'ers say you do at actively involving them?
   a. excellent
   b. fair
   c. poor

1b. **(for X'ers only):**
How good of a job does your manager do at actively involving you?
   a. excellent
   b. fair
   c. poor

2. What are three potential barriers to actively involving X'ers in the design, implementation, and evaluation of job-relevant business processes?

   1. ______________________________

   2. ______________________________

   3. ______________________________

3. What are two problems associated with employee suggestion systems and two effective ways to address these shortcomings?

Problems

1. ______________________________

2. ______________________________

Solutions

1. ______________________________

2. ______________________________

4. Name three specific things a manager can do to provide Active Involvement for X'ers with regard to making them an instrumental part of the decision-making process?

1. ______________________________

2. ______________________________

3. ______________________________

5. List three specific ways to effectively challenge X'ers:

1. ______________________________

2. ______________________________

3. ______________________________

6. List three specific ways to create a fun working environment for X'ers:

   1. ______________________________

   2. ______________________________

   3. ______________________________

5

Top Ten Ways to De-Motivate X'ers

10. Take all the credit for a project they spent three weeks on.
9. Never say "thank you," "nice work" or "I appreciate the effort."
8. Pass them by on promotions for fear they will get too big for their britches.
7. Refrain from smiling.
6. Forget to give them a raise three years in a row.
5. Tell them that they are easily replaceable.
4. Pay older employees more for doing the same exact work.
3. Dwell on the negatives.
2. Give them a company-logoed plastic paper clip holder for winning the Employee of the Month award.
1. Let graying senior executives decide what young people will find motivating.

X'ers-Gone-Entrepreneurs
Cleveland, OH

GIVING CREDIT WHERE CREDIT IS DUE

"With recognition, you're trying to prevent employees from rationalizing that it's OK to do anything less than a quality job."

Hedy Gruenebaum Abromovitz and Les Abromovitz in *Bringing TQM on the QT to Your Organization*

"Everyone needs to feel that their contributions are noticed. The work we do and the recognition we get for it contribute to our self-esteem."

Jan Carlzon in *Moments of Truth*

While seniority and experience still have their place in most organizations, members of the X-workforce feel they primarily deserve rewards and reinforcement based on their achievements and proven talents. **The third component of the NAKED model, Key Recognition, is rooted in the concept of meritocracy.** Invariably, the X-Generation's inclination to buck the "work your way up the ladder" mentality causes friction and generational perception problems with many managers. But acknowledging X-er's hard work and achievements positively affects their morale, company loyalty, and subsequent levels of performance. Managers additionally benefit because X'ers' success reflects favorably upon *them*. In essence, sharing the limelight with X'ers establishes a mutually winning situation.

Implementing Key Recognition at a basic level consists of giving promotions, raises, and achievement or service awards to deserving X'ers. Managers must ensure that these decisions are based on specific and objective criteria, not on subjective whims. For instance, Employee of the Month programs rely on company politics and favoritism when no clear nomination and selection guidelines exist. Standardizing procedures helps to diminish bias and promotes a higher code of fairness for giving credit where credit is due.

The X-workforce can improve the process of Key Recognition by gaining a better understanding of the criteria for it. Similar to studying for a test, knowing exactly what it will take to "make the grade" is imperative. Bonus structures, job succession tracks, and performance awards are a perfect match for achievement-oriented X'ers.

POSITIVE PAYS OFF

"...you build up self-esteem by accentuating positive experiences. It's like making deposits into a bank account. Every time you have a positive interaction with somebody, for example, and you catch that person doing something right and praise him or her, it's like putting money in their self-esteem account. If you and that person are able to make enough positive deposits, when the going gets tough and that person needs inner strength to draw upon, there is something in the account."

Excerpt from *The Power of Ethical Management* by Ken Blanchard and Norman Vincent Peale

Many managers resort to negative reinforcement to achieve their goals. Their rationale is that people will perform stated objectives (e.g., meeting project deadlines), to avoid undesirable consequences. According to this theory, the threat of losing special privileges, prided responsibilities, and ultimately their jobs will keep the majority of employees in line.

With regard to the X-workforce, though, forced compliance, intimidation tactics, and punishment produce strictly short-term results. As one regretful manager points out:

"What I have found to be true over the last couple of years is that there is a new breed of young workers. These are guys who don't want to play the line-staff game anymore. It's like they're fed up or something. They stand up in defiance when you yell at them or threaten to dock their pay. They're not scared to tell you to go take a hike."

Steve, 39 — lead supervisor at automotive center in Orlando, FL

Managing with clenched fists has limited utility with the X-workforce. It shrivels morale and fosters a groundswell of resentment. X'ers refuse to tolerate bosses who come across as tyrants or total jerks.

If managers do not like what they see when they scrutinize the X-Generation's work ethic, they *especially* must take the concept of Key Recognition to heart. This means using *positive* reinforcement to motivate X'ers instead of punishment or the avoidance of painful consequences. Rewarding and publicly acknowledging members of the X-Generation for following the rules and meeting performance goals is a sure bet when properly executed. Successful outcomes include a significant turnaround in X'er productivity, job satisfaction, confidence, loyalty, and commitment to tasks.

One informal way to give positive Key Recognition to X'ers is praise. Depending on the situation, it can be given in small or large doses. It has to be specific and must immediately follow the desired behavior or it will lose its value as a reinforcer. Saying "thank you" or "nice job" are easy ways for managers to show their appreciation for X'ers' contributions. While these ideas are simplistic and intuitively obvious, most managers rarely apply them.

X'ers, in comparison, need to show managers that positive reinforcement has a reciprocal flow. Managers never hear "thank you" or "nice job" from members of the X-Generation either. The two-way street paradigm must transcend hierarchical boundaries. Key Recognition suggestions for X'ers include sending a short memo or a thank you note to their bosses when they deserve it. Managers are always astounded, yet deeply grateful, when X'ers share their positive sentiments.

NAKED SUCCESS: PROFILE OF A **NATIONSBANK** X'ER

Company: **NATIONSBANK**
Industry: Banking
Headquarters: Charlotte, North Carolina

Key Facts: The people at NationsBank have a common goal — to be the premier financial services company in the United States. NationsBank is one of the largest companies in the industry already, well known for its capital strength, market position, and bias for doing business in all sectors of the communities it serves. Through its broad retail banking activities, NationsBank serves more than 8 million households and businesses. Its general bank, with almost 2,000 locations, has representation throughout the Southeast, Southwest, and Mid-Atlantic states. NationsBank is also a socially responsible company, as demonstrated through its $100 million affordable housing fund and established creative partnerships with community-based organizations such as the NAACP and the National Urban League. The success of the company is rooted in the empowerment of all its employees, and is characterized by Hugh McColl Jr., chairman and chief executive officer of NationsBank, as "leadership, teamwork and winning...in a world of ongoing challenges."

> *"NationsBank is a true meritocracy—you get what you earn. Hard work pays off here."*

Name: Donnamarie
Title: Banking Center Manager
Age: 29

Tenure/History: Donna started in banking as a teller at age 17. After working for several banks, she decided to go back to school to get her finance degree. Upon graduation, she was hired into the NationsBank management development program. By age 27, Donna was managing a bank. Only eight months later, she was made an officer of the bank. Then, at 29, her manager insisted that she was ready for a greater challenge and promoted her to banking center manager at a facility of much larger physical size, market scope, number of staff, and deposit base.

Motivating Things About Her Job: *"Making decisions here feels so comfortable. We have a whole recognition program — Freedom to Act — built around it. We call the actual bank we work in a 'banking center,' not just a 'branch.' My self-esteem needs get met."*

Motivating Things About Her Boss: *"I don't like anyone standing over my shoulder. My boss is never hovering over me to make sure I get the work done. It's all based on trust — and I like to be trusted. Nelson gives me lots of room to grow. The check and balance is our daily reports, and that is a good thing. My boss is not physically in my face, but he is always in the loop."*

What Keeps Her From Leaving: *"The company supports you from the top down. When they say they believe in empowerment and recognition, they really mean it. I get rewarded for making the calls, not reprimanded. I see a huge future for me here. I want to represent this company at the national level and earn the Hugh McColl executive award."*

Most Memorable "Naked Moment": *"When our general banking president rolled out the Freedom to Act recognition program for empowerment, it was unbelievable. He went to each state and every region to do launch seminars — he made it clear that this was not a bunch of lip service."*

THE CARROT AND THE STICK

> *"Manage results, not just activities....Every contest should have a "carrot" and a "stick." Reward the people who achieve the incentive goals and retrain the ones who don't....The "stick" is for moving them along the right path, not for beating their backsides."*
>
> Jim Sullivan and Phil Roberts in *Service that Sells!: The Art of Profitable Hospitality*

The application of tangible reinforcement with X'ers further augments the power of Key Recognition. This is especially true for X'ers who are more extrinsically than intrinsically motivated. Knowing that there is something in it for them — the "carrot" — sparks their enthusiasm to produce results. Money, prizes, stock, special awards, vacations, and celebrations all constitute concrete rewards that may make X'ers feel vindicated and appreciated for their hard work. In his book, *1001 Ways to Reward Employees,* Bob Nelson provides ample coverage of the full arsenal of "carrots" managers have at their disposal.

The practical utility of tangible Key Recognition is greatest when members of the X-Generation are rewarded for small chunks of goal-directed behaviors. Managers need to gauge how much X'ers can realistically accomplish, then set performance goals and select the appropriate incentives. Each correctly elicited action must be reinforced with desirable consequences. For example, boosting X'er productivity can entail issuing them prizes for meeting deadlines. The overriding philosophy boils down to setting up a successful strategy where productivity goals — the "stick" — and X'er Key Recognition needs get met.

An additional facet of tangible Key Recognition is that X'ers have to let managers know when the "carrot" is too loosely tied to the end of the "stick." In other words, when incentives are inadequately linked to job performance. If an X'er's productivity shows significant gains but continues to go "unrecognized," then it is up to that individual to get the situation properly addressed. Members of the X-Generation also must alert managers to the feasibility of the goals they are asked to achieve. To avoid becoming overwhelmed and frustrated, they X'ers to make managers aware of the pace at which they can be pushed.

NAKED SUCCESS: PROFILE OF A **DRYCLEAN-U.S.A.** X'ER

Company: **DRYCLEAN-U.S.A.**
Industry: Drycleaning
Headquarters: Fort Lauderdale, Florida

Key Facts: In 1976, Dryclean-U.S.A. opened its first store in Coral Gables, Florida. Through aggressive franchising, Dryclean-U.S.A. is now trying to become *the* dominant dry cleaning operation in a $4 billion domestic industry. The key to Dryclean-U.S.A.'s success is consistent marketing and the creation of a uniform look in its stores, advertising, and approach to customers. In 1988, the chain was purchased by Johnson Group Cleaners PLC of Liverpool, England, the world's largest dry cleaners owner of more than 1,200 stores. Dryclean-U.S.A. itself currently has over 100 outlets in South Florida alone. Overall, the company has well over 300 stores and is expanding throughout the United States and into Central and South America. Some of the most recent store openings have been in Guatemala, Mexico, Chile, and Ecuador. Other domestic locations where Dryclean-U.S.A. has a presence include Arizona, California, Georgia, Maryland, Massachusetts, New York, North Carolina, Ohio, Pennsylvania, South Carolina, Texas, Virginia, Washington, and Wisconsin.

> *"I love being part of the team here — my manager is a big part of that team."*

Name: Evelina
Title: Counter Person
Age: 19

Tenure/History: Evelina, whose primary work experience had been bussing tables in various restaurants, started working for Dryclean-U.S.A. upon moving to Florida at age 18. Somewhat reluctant to work in the dry cleaning industry (she knew very little about it upon taking the job), Evelina learned quickly and was pleasantly surprised by how much she actually enjoyed working for Felisa, one of Dryclean-U.S.A.'s top store managers. Evelina, per Felisa's glowing testimony, has shown tremendous progress and now knows how to do virtually everything in the store. Between tagging, racking, and bagging incoming clothes, in addition to operating the cash register, and providing impeccable service in a fast-paced environment, she has grown to be a major asset not only to her manager, her co-workers, and the company, but to her loyal customers as well.

Motivating Things About Her Job: *"I like working with the customers, my co-workers and especially my boss. It makes my job seem easy and fun. I never thought I'd say that I like working at a dry cleaner, but I do. The only tough part was learning the computer and the procedures. This really is a great place."*

Motivating Things About Her Boss: *"Felisa is genuinely a good person. She consistently treats people well, and she treats each one of us the same way. Felisa talks to me like I'm her friend, not just her employee. She even makes an effort to be nice to my family. What I like about Felisa is that she is very approachable and easy to talk to. She truly seems to understand what it's all about for me."*

What Keeps Her From Leaving: *"Not only do I like my job, I like working for Felisa. I don't think I'll ever find another manager as good as her, no matter where I go. She is definitely the best manager I have ever had. I plan to stay here."*

Most Memorable "Naked Moment": *"One afternoon a woman came in and we were already closed. I let her drop off her clothes anyway, because I know Felisa trusts me to make my own decisions and use my best judgment. The next day the same woman came in and brought me a huge box of gift-wrapped candy. I was happy to have gone the extra mile for her, even without the gift. And I knew that Felisa would be happy — not upset like other managers I have had — that I bent the rules. Felisa would do the same herself to help a customer."*

THE DESIRABILITY FACTOR

"...reward systems must be tailored to individual needs if they are to enhance the quality of work life. People's needs determine the kinds of rewards that are valued. Because employees can differ widely in what rewards they want, reward systems must be designed to recognize those individual differences."

Thomas G. Cummings and Edgar F.Huse in *Organization Development and Change*

Key Recognition mismatches can be fatal. For instance, a Salesperson of the Month program which awards winners a $200 gold-plated pen set will backfire if what recipients really want is a cash bonus or gift certificate to spend as they wish. The problem is that managers rarely take the time — or have the interest — to ask X'ers what motivates *them*. The X-workforce's idea of a powerful incentive may deeply contrast managers' historical assumptions.

Often the things which entice members of the X-Generation the most are inexpensive, according to the countless X'ers interviewed for this book. For some X'ers, simply having a set of their own official business cards or getting their job title changed from "front desk clerk" to "personal sales associate" is significant. Others insist that having a nameplate on their desk or a personalized memo pad is a tremendous perk. Pride, for X'ers, is an extremely important aspect of the satisfaction equation. It directly relates to their overall morale and job commitment.

Additional reinforcers that many X'ers say motivate them include concert and sporting event seats, movie tickets, days off with pay, bar tabs, dinner-for-two coupons, CDs, and "fun money" for video rentals and groceries. Cash, contrary to what some managers believe, is one of the top items on X'ers' list of desired rewards, even if it is not a million dollars. In the Economy from Hell, money is a scarce and highly demanded commodity which rivals non-negotiable prizes.

X'ers also like novelty in Key Recognition. Games, competitions, and contests can by themselves be attractive forms of Key Recognition. If these events are fun, creative, and have a lot of chances to win, X'ers will be excited to participate. Periodically changing the prizes helps to prevent their gradual disinterest and boredom (or lack of challenge!). By making Key Recognition enjoyable, exciting, dynamic, and desirable, X'ers have one more reason to work hard, and one less excuse to leave.

Finally, X'ers must clearly identify for themselves what is motivating. Reflecting on those incentives which have personally worked for them in the past is a logical starting point. It is then their responsibility to tell their managers — as much as it is their managers' task to ask them — which rewards are most desirable and successfully reinforcing.

NAKED CHECKLIST: KEY RECOGNITION

Fulfillment of each of the following tasks is a key aspect of implementing Naked Management as it relates to this chapter. The listed items for managers and X'ers may be added to or revised to fit individual work environments or company policies.

For Managers:

___ 1. ***Utilize the concept of meritocracy when giving Key Recognition to X'ers.*** Reward them based on their achievements and proven talents. Give credit where credit is due.

___ 2. ***Issue promotions, monetary raises, and service awards to deserving X'ers.*** Ensure that these decisions are based on specific and objective criteria, not on subjective whims. Standardize procedures to diminish bias.

___ 3. ***Use positive reinforcement to motivate X'ers.*** Reward them and publicly acknowledge them. Give them context-specific praise immediately following desired behaviors. Always remember to say thank you when you appreciate an X'er's contributions.

___ 4. ***Tangibly and systematically reinforce X'ers' goal-directed behaviors.*** Let them know that there potentially *is* something in it for them (the "carrot"). Use concrete rewards like money, prizes, stock, special awards, vacations, and celebrations. The practical utility of these incentives is greatest when they are solidly linked to tangible behavioral goals (the "stick").

___ 5. ***Teach X'ers small, digestible chunks of behavior.*** Reinforce each correctly elicited action with desirable consequences. Gauge how much X'ers can realistically accomplish, then set performance goals and select the appropriate incentives.

___ 6. ***Ask X'ers about the types of incentives that they want.*** Rewards X'ers often say are desirable include personalized memo pads and business cards, better job titles, concert and sporting event seats, movie tickets, paid days off, dinner coupons, bar tabs, CDs, "fun money" for groceries or video rentals, and cash. Provide novelty and fun through games and competitions.

For X'ers:

___ 1. ***Know the measures by which your performance is judged.*** Find out exactly what it takes to get Key Recognition. Check into the criteria used for bonus structures, performance awards, and job promotion tracks.

___ 2. ***Show managers that positive reinforcement has a reciprocal flow.*** Express gratitude, tell them congratulations on their special accomplishments and send them short memos or thank you notes when they are warranted. Keep in mind that Key Recognition is a two-way street.

___ 3. ***Provide managers with any information that will allow them to evaluate the effectiveness or "fit" of reward systems and performance goals.*** Let them know when incentives are inadequately tied to job success criteria. Alert them to the size of the "small chunks" of behavior which best align with your personal learning style and pace.

___ 4. ***Identify for yourself what is motivating, then let managers know.*** Start by reflecting on those incentives which have worked for you in the past. It is your responsibility, too, to identify rewards which entice you.

X'ERCISE 5: WHAT MAKES 'EM TICK

DIRECTIONS

The following items are designed to help you assess your strategy for putting the NAKED Model component "**K**ey Recognition" into practice. Write your answers in the spaces provided or on a separate sheet of paper. Then, discuss your responses with other managers and/or X'ers.

1a. **(for managers only):**
How good of a job would your X'ers say you do at providing them with Key Recognition?
   a. excellent
   b. fair
   c. poor

1b. **(for X'ers only):**
How good of a job does your manager do at providing you with Key Recognition?
   a. excellent
   b. fair
   c. poor

2. Name three potential problems that can arise from using Key Recognition with X'ers:

   1. ______________________________

   2. ______________________________

   3. ______________________________

3. Name four rules of thumb for using Key Recognition with X'ers:

    1. ______________________________

    2. ______________________________

    3. ______________________________

    4. ______________________________

4. As an "X'periment," ask several managers **and** X'ers what specific types of Key Recognition are most motivating **to X'ers**. List five responses from each group and then compare:

    What Managers Said

    1. ______________________________

    2. ______________________________

    3. ______________________________

    4. ______________________________

    5. ______________________________

    What X'ers Said

    1. ______________________________

    2. ______________________________

    3. ______________________________

    4. ______________________________

    5. ______________________________

6

Top Ten Things X'ers Want to Tell Workaholic Managers

10. All work and no play can be hazardous to your health.
9. The company would save a lot of money on electricity if you turned off your office light before 9 p.m. each night.
8. Don't worry about us, it's not like we have a social life or anything.
7. Maybe you haven't heard about the latest fad called *stress management*.
6. Perfection is overrated.
5. There is something about daylight that you just come to miss.
4. Burnout: a condition achieved by forgetting that work is only one part of life.
3. Is it Halloween, or do you *like* having a pale face and dark rings under your eyes?
2. Get a hobby.
1. Even God took a day off.

Quality of Worklife Committee
Madison, WI

WHAT DO YOU MEAN YOU'VE GOT A LIFE?

"Xers value their time away from work.... They were the first latch-key kids to hit the workforce, and many of them resent the amount of time their parents spent at work. As a result, Xers with families have decided to put their family before their job. They are determined to spend more time with their children and spouses than their parents did. To them, work is what you do so you can have a life.

Shannon O'Brien in *"X Marks the Spot: How will Generation X Affect Your Firm?"*

Most managers today know the value of a hard day's work. They have paid their dues and learned the ropes like those who held similar positions before them. Getting to this level did not come easy. It took long hours, years of experience, and sometimes even waiting in line. Their modi operandi was, and continues to be, *"Don't quit until the job is done."* Like their parents, many of whom worked six or seven days a week, from dawn until dusk, these managers show tremendous pride in their career accomplishments, proven sticktuitiveness, and unwavering work ethic. To them, the company and their supervisory role in it have always come first. Life is work, and work becomes life: seldom is there a clear separation between the two.

Given this perspective, it becomes easier to see why some managers have little respect nor tolerance for how many X'ers view the concept of work.

In general, the X-workforce is predominantly concerned with quality of life issues. Balance in life and work is viewed as the key to happiness. As a result, *"carpe diem"* ("seize the day") prevails as the rule of thumb. According to research cited by Helen Wilkinson in an article in *The Guardian, "...higher-educated Generation X-ers are defining a new work ethic, based on balance and fulfillment, strikingly different from the Protestant work ethic."*

X'ers want immediate gratification. They do not readily buy into company politics and bureaucratic red tape. They choose to spend dedicated time with their friends and families above staying late to finish a project. To them, personal sacrifice at work is "out," while self-preservation is "in." The classic workaholism that engulfed *their* parents is no longer acceptable. Total investment of oneself in the company seems pointless, if not foolish, to most X'ers.

Empathy, the fourth component of the NAKED Model, strengthens the working relationship between managers and X'ers by promoting a culture of understanding, caring, and genuine interest in each other's respective problems and viewpoints. In practical terms, Empathy means putting oneself in another's shoes. X'ers want managers to recognize that they *do* have a life, and to convey that awareness through their attitudes and actions. Mary Ann Sieghart, in her story in *The Times,* suggests that *"...managers should be flexible; to judge employees by their output, not by the number of hours they spend behind their desks."*

Some concrete interventions for facilitating this type of active Empathy at the managerial level consist of flexible scheduling or flextime, telecommuting programs, shift rotation, four-day work weeks, compensation time, and job sharing. These techniques take into account X'ers' specific circumstances and the context of those situations (e.g., school schedules, pregnancy, vacations, overtime, young children at home, social life, illness). Managers, taking into account any reluctance they may have, need to put in place systemic changes and new ideas which demonstrate their concern for the well-being of their X'ers.

Active Empathy also needs to be demonstrated by members of the X-workforce. Going out of their way to make a manager's load a little lighter, not taking vacation days during peak periods, and assisting their supervisors in the creation of a more Empathy-focused working environment are all potent examples which the X-Generation can utilize to everyone's mutual benefit. Essentially, X'ers must look at managers' concerns as if they were their own.

NAKED SUCCESS: PROFILE OF A **KINKO'S** X'ER

Company: **KINKO'S**
Industry: Photocopying/Business Services
Headquarters: Ventura, California

Key Facts: In 1970, Paul Orfalea, affectionately known as "Kinko" because of his curly red hair, opened his first store selling school supplies and copies in the small college town of Isla Vista, near the University of California, Santa Barbara. The original store was only 100 square feet and featured a single copier. Today, there are more than 800 Kinko's locations worldwide. There are stores in every state in the United States, in addition to representation in Canada, Japan, South Korea, and the Netherlands. Internally, the Kinko's culture stresses respect and concern for fellow co-workers. There is minimal hierarchy and clear guidelines (the 14 "Commitments to Communication") for how co-workers must treat one another. The company philosophy emphasizes people's need to live balanced lives in work, love, and play. Kinko's is committed to providing products and services that help them approach their communication needs more efficiently and effectively. From color to black and white copies to computer rentals, videoconferencing, electronic document distribution, and overnight drop-off services, Kinko's provides business service solutions that consistently fulfill its promise as *The New Way To Office*SM.

> *"I'm here because I feel I'm needed. My manager makes it clear to me that I am an essential part of what goes on here."*

Name: Tien
Title: Assistant Manager
Age: 22

Tenure/History: At age 15, Tien began his working career at his father's gas station. From there he did temporary stints in a baseball card shop, fast food restaurants, and the landscaping business in order to make money while going to school. Tien first came to Kinko's a year and one half ago as a part-time co-worker while attending college in Mobile, Alabama. Thinking this was just one more short-term job, he was pleasantly surprised to find that he liked working for Kinko's, especially for Byron, his manager. After only four months, Tien was promoted to assistant manager. Byron, who had become a friend of Tien's, was soon transferred to South Florida as store manager of a larger Kinko's Branch Office. Two months later, Byron called Tien and told him there was an opening for assistant manager. Tien, jumping on the opportunity to work for Byron in one of the highest volume stores in the region, came to Florida where he plans to finish his college degree.

Motivating Things About His Job: *"When I come to work, I always see things that can be done. There is room to make improvements. It is not the kind of job where you dread coming to work. I like it here. I especially like dealing with the customers. My goal is to get to the next level in Kinko's — I want to move up. And in this company, you can do just that."*

Motivating Things About His Boss: *"What I like most about Byron is his work ethic. What I mean by this is that there is nothing he would make his co-workers do that he would not do himself. He is a very positive person, and I have come to know him as a friend. He is good about giving us the big picture and keeping us posted on our individual and team progress on a regular basis. He lets us know what we need to do to hit our goals and spells out the rewards we will get in return."*

What Keeps Him From Leaving: *"I still work here because I like this job and who I work for. There are a lot of opportunities available to me in this company. Plus, I get a lot of respect from my boss and my co-workers. I would not be here if I did not like it as much as I do. Instead, I would find something I enjoy more. There is no sense in hating your job."*

Most Memorable "Naked Moment": *"One day a customer came in hysterically crying. She needed help on a major project that needed to go out that afternoon. The papers were crumpled, and some of them were wet from the rain. First, I gave her a tissue and let her re-group. Then I told her I would try to make it look better. It turned out great. Later she came back to thank me — now smiling. I was able to make a positive difference in a customer's life."*

EMPATHY VS. SYMPATHY

> *"It is easy to confuse empathy with sympathy, but the concepts are different in two important ways. First, sympathy means you feel compassion for another person's predicament, whereas empathy means you have a personal sense of what that predicament is like....Empathy is different from sympathy in another way. We only sympathize when we accept the reasons for another's pain as valid, whereas it's possible to empathize without feeling sympathy....Empathizing allows you to understand another person's motives without requiring you to agree with them."*
>
> Ron Adler and Neil Towne in *Looking Out/Looking In*

Based on the marked difference in the way X'ers and managers think about work, Empathy is a desperately needed, yet greatly misunderstood, tool. The main problem is that most people see Empathy as being synonymous with sympathy. They believe that having Empathy insinuates feeling sorry for others, agreeing with everything they say, applauding their lifestyle and supporting all of their choices. They view it as an across-the-board endorsement; a testament of their undying compassion or pity for someone else. By showing Empathy, they perceive that they are giving up the very ground they stand on, violating their highest principles and reducing themselves to nothing more than other-advocates.

For instance, most managers are astute enough to see the constrictive and demoralizing effects of the Economy from Hell on X'ers. Nevertheless, they may look at shrinking job opportunities as simply one more obstacle along the bumpy road of life. Certainly, they know it must be tough for members of the X-workforce. But in their view, no one ever has had it easy in the beginning. They look to their own personal experience of starting out and working up the ladder, then conclude: "Same stuff, different day. X'ers must play with the cards they were dealt and get over it." It may not occur to these managers, nor matter, that there have been significant changes in the issues facing young people over the last 25 to 50 years.

The missing piece in this routine scenario is the *human* element. Managers, despite their possible disinterest in the gory details of X'er plight and misfortune, need to demonstrate that they at least are trying to relate to the troubling situations in which X'ers find themselves. They have to step outside their microcosms and enter the psyche of the X-Generation in a sincere attempt to identify with X'ers' prevailing thoughts and values. Nowhere are managers required to *sympathize* with X'ers or give them their stamp of approval. They must simply communicate to X'ers their genuine understanding:

> *"My X'ers love it when they see me pitching in on the front lines. They also cherish the fact that I treat them like real people. I try my best to look at issues from their point of view. My goal is to take an open-minded yet objective approach to being a manager. It's the only way to let people know that you believe in them."*
>
> Rachel, 41 — store manager for commercial printer in Charleston, SC

Authenticity is a non-negotiable element of Empathy. X'ers can smell phoniness from a mile away. It is critical that managers be true to themselves as well as to X'ers in their attempts to convey understanding and appear "real." Anything else is counter-productive and potentially disastrous.

Additional Empathy skills and techniques which managers can use to make interpersonal connections with the X-workforce — without having to be sympathetic — include taking an active role in team activities and tasks, accommodating scheduling requests whenever possible, showing sincere concern for X'ers' welfare, encouraging X'ers to pursue outside interests, and respecting X'ers for who they are (not for whom managers want them to be). Moreover, when managers feel comfortable talking about mistakes that *they* personally made in the past and the subsequent learnings that followed, their credibility with members of the X-Generation skyrockets.

It is also imperative that members of the X-workforce show managers the Empathy to which they are rightfully entitled. This does not necessitate compassion, only fundamental caring and positive regard. It is the reciprocity of gut-level understanding and interpersonal warmth which allows managers and X'ers to forge positive working relationships.

AN EARFUL GOES A LONG WAY

> *"'Seek first to understand' involves a very deep shift in paradigm. We typically seek first to be understood. Most people do not listen with the intent to understand; they listen with the intent to reply. They're either speaking or preparing to speak. They're filtering everything through their own paradigms, reading their autobiography into other people's lives. ...Empathic listening is so powerful because it gives you accurate data to work with. Instead of projecting your own autobiography and assuming thoughts, feelings, motives and*

interpretation, you're dealing with the reality inside another person's head and heart. You're listening to understand. You're focused on receiving the deep communication of another human soul."

Stephen Covey in *The 7 Habits of Highly Effective People*

Good listening skills are an essential part of Empathy. X'ers need to know that the things they tell their managers matter. Likewise, it is important for them to be able to say what is on their mind without fear of imminent repercussions. They want to feel valued and *truly* heard, not ignored or superficially placated. Managers, if they are trying to be empathetic, have to talk less and listen more. They must help X'ers feel safe in coming to them with their problems.

When managers take this nonjudgmental approach with the X-workforce, they effectively set up an environment conducive to the positive exchange of thoughts and ideas. X'ers, consequently, begin to feel comfortable using them as a sounding board instead of looking at them as a judge and jury. Managers' accessibility and skill in empathic listening are primary factors in cultivating X'er morale and productivity. They add needed credibility to typically hypocritical "open-door" policies.

Basic hands-on listening techniques for managers include acknowledging X'ers with a friendly and sincere greeting (as opposed to pretending they are not there), showing respect for them as human beings (regardless of how young or inexperienced they are), withholding judgment (whether agreeing with them or not), and using body language to convey genuine interest in what they are saying (e.g., leaning forward and keeping eye contact). Other beneficial empathic listening practices consist of asking them relevant questions, paraphrasing their remarks, and showing them respect while they are talking (e.g., not interrupting, pseudolistening, nor rummaging through files).

Conversely, X'ers must make a concerted effort to hone their own listening skills. A major complaint from managers is that the X-workforce maintains a universal *"I don't care about anyone but myself"* attitude. This breeds further X'erism and contempt from managers. Members of the X-Generation need to let their supervisors know that they take their jobs seriously and are prepared to listen and share ideas. In cases where X'ers feel neglected or ignored, they must take it upon themselves to meet with their managers to discuss the precipitating issues.

NAKED SUCCESS : PROFILE OF A **MIRAGE** X'ER

Company: **MIRAGE RESORTS INCORPORATED**
Industry: Hotel and Gaming
Headquarters: Las Vegas, Nevada

Key Facts: Mirage Resorts Inc. owns and operates several of the most renowned hotel and gaming establishments in the world: The Mirage, Treasure Island, the Golden Nugget Las Vegas and the Golden Nugget in Laughlin, Nevada. In the near future, the company will add two more major theme properties on the Las Vegas Strip. The Mirage is widely known for its on-site volcano which explodes every 15 minutes along with its luxurious gaming, tropical theme, fine dining, white tiger and dolphin exhibits, and tantalizing Siegfried & Roy show. Treasure Island also spotlights an exciting pirate sea-battle attraction and twice-nightly presentations of Cirque du Soleil's fascinating performance, Mystère. All of Mirage Resorts' properties are huge successes, both with guests and employees. They stand out as the more popular and highly visited establishments and boast some of the industry's lowest staff turnover figures. A potent combination of bold and consistent leadership, superior quality, breakthrough marketing and unprecedented caring for over 18,000 employees helps put this company at the top.

> *"I like working hard in this place because I am allowed to enjoy life while I am here."*

Name: Amie
Title: Room Reservation Clerk
Age: 25

Tenure/History: At age 20, Amie came to The Mirage after brief tenure at other Las Vegas properties. Starting off as a retail cashier, she was promoted within a year to the front desk. For the next two and one-half years, Amie diligently worked and demonstrated her strengths as a loyal employee. When Treasure Island at the Mirage opened in fall 1993, she moved over to the new property as a room reservations clerk. Just a little more than one year later,

Amie was formally recognized as the 1994 Treasure Island Employee of the Year. Currently, she is aiming toward her next step up in the company.

Motivating Things About Her Job: *"This company treats you very well. The benefits are great, and the managers are fair. Everyone is very friendly and tries to work as a team. Managers treat you like an equal and are on your level. They respect you and understand you. If you have a problem, you can go to them. You don't have to be afraid."*

Motivating Things About Her Boss: *"My supervisor Annette is like my mentor. She supports me in everything I do, even if it means moving to a different department in the company. If there is something on my mind, she makes herself available both at work and outside work. That shows a lot of caring. She knows how to say the right things and put life in perspective."*

What Keeps Her From Leaving: *"It is the casual yet professional atmosphere. You can't take life too seriously. I know my supervisor truly cares about my welfare. She wants me to take care of myself if I am sick. She tries to accommodate me when I need time off. She is there for me during the tough times. Annette is my boss, but she is also like family to me."*

Most Memorable "Naked Moment": *"When I won the Employee of the Year Award, I truly felt like a star. I am still beaming from the thrill of it. I will never forget when my award was presented to me by former President and First Lady George and Barbara Bush. All my life, my dream was to come to this great country to live and work. My second dream was to meet an American president. I cherish that moment and the photograph I have of it."*

WHERE THE RUBBER MEETS THE ROAD

"How sad! .. 'people stuff' had come to be looked at as 'soft.' But though business schools may deny it, and corporate leader after corporate leader may neglect it, 'they,' the people in the remote distribution center in Dubuque or Fairbanks, the people cleaning the streets, schooling the young or frying the burgers are what it's all about, what it has always been about, and what it always will be about. Make no mistake about it. 'Techniques' don't produce quality products, educate children, or pick up the garbage on time: people do, people who care, people who are treated as creatively contributing adults."

Tom Peters and Nancy Austin in
A Passion for Excellence

Although Empathy is often considered an intangible notion, the bottom line on Empathy is very palpable and real. There are associated costs and benefits with being a good listener and conveying genuine understanding. On the downside, managers cannot be available for X'ers 100% of the day. Their good intentions to spend quality moments with their staffs are easily deterred by spontaneous meetings, emerging crises, and other competing priorities.

Patience represents another challenge for managers. When there are mounting deadlines and countless fires to put out, showing Empathy for the X-workforce may plummet on the list of priorities. Not only is there less time to attentively listen to anyone's concerns, the probability of losing one's temper dramatically increases. Before long, the guiding premise of Empathy can get lost in the shuffle.

In light of these issues, the return on investment with Empathy is significant. When managers convey warmth and understanding, the result is greater X-workforce dependability (e.g., being on time, low usage of sick days), new respect for managers and the company, higher morale and job satisfaction, better teamwork, and quality performance. X'ers' motivation, productivity, and loyalty are augmented when they perceive their managers to be attentive, down-to-earth, and committed to the individuals on their team:

"It's been seven years that I'm working here now. Most people move from place to place, back and forth, no real loyalty as I see it. Except at this dealership. It's the GM who's responsible for it. He's the guy who is always there to share a laugh or get a burger with you at

lunch if you need to talk. He's the reason why I've turned down offers from our competition down the street."

Pete, 28 — assistant sales manager at automobile dealership in Biloxi, MS

An additional payoff is that members of the X-workforce invariably go the extra mile for bosses who show them Empathy. This includes meeting tight deadlines, taking on extra projects, heading up impromptu projects, assisting in event planning, volunteering for overtime and even staying late or coming in early when there is a clear need for it. X'ers do not buy into obsessive workaholism, but they will more than shoulder their load if they have a truly empathetic manager. It is a matter of pride, reciprocation and making sure that what goes around actually does come around.

NAKED CHECKLIST: EMPATHY

Fulfillment of each of the following tasks is a key aspect of implementing Naked Management as it relates to this chapter. The listed items for managers and X'ers may be added to or revised to fit individual work environments or company policies.

For Managers:

___ 1. ***Use Empathy to promote a culture of understanding, caring, and genuine interest in what X'ers have to say.*** Try to put yourself in their shoes.

___ 2. ***Recognize that X'ers do have a life.*** Convey this through your attitudes and actions. Concrete interventions for facilitating this type of Empathy include X'er telecommuting programs, flexible scheduling or flextime, shift rotation, four-day work weeks, compensation time, and job sharing.

___ 3. ***Utilize informal Empathy techniques to create solid interpersonal connections with the X-workforce — this does not require having sympathy for them.*** Take an active role in team activities, be flexible with scheduling requests, show genuine concern for X'ers' welfare, encourage them to pursue outside interests, and respect them for who they are. Talk about mistakes *you* made in the past and how you learned from them. Most of all, be human.

___ 4. ***Take a nonjudgmental approach to interactions with the X-workforce.*** Become a sounding board, not a judge and jury. Make yourself available and accessible to discuss performance-related issues. Give credibility back to "open door" policies.

___ 5. ***Implement hands-on, practical listening techniques.*** Acknowledge X'ers with a sincere greeting, use body language to convey genuine interest (e.g., lean forward, nod your head, keep eye contact, ask relevant questions, paraphrase or summarize their remarks, don't interrupt) and give them your undivided attention when they are talking. Give them quality time.

For X'ers:

___ 1. ***Use Empathy to promote a culture of understanding, caring, and genuine interest in what managers have to say.*** Try to put yourself in their shoes.

___ 2. ***Go out of your way to make your manager's load lighter.*** Take fewer high peak vacation days and do your part to help create an empathic working environment. Look at managers' concerns as if they were your own.

___ 3. ***Remember that managers are real people too.*** Show them gut-level understanding, a fundamental sense of caring, warmth, and positive regard.

___ 4. ***Make a concerted effort to hone your listening skills.*** Let managers know that you take your job seriously and that you are ready to listen and share ideas. If you feel neglected or ignored, bring it up with your supervisor.

X'ERCISE 6: IN THEIR SHOES

DIRECTIONS

The following items are designed to help you assess your strategy for putting the NAKED Model component "**E**mpathy" into practice. Write your answers in the spaces provided or on a separate sheet of paper. Then, discuss your responses with other managers and/or X'ers.

1a. **(for managers only):**
How good of a job would your X'ers say you do at showing them Empathy?
   a. excellent
   b. fair
   c. poor

1b. **(for X'ers only):**
How good of a job does your manager do at showing you Empathy?
   a. excellent
   b. fair
   c. poor

2. Name three specific situations in which X'ers can be shown empathy without giving them sympathy:

   1. ______________________________

   2. ______________________________

   3. ______________________________

3. Name five listening skills that both managers and X'ers need to have to more effectively convey Empathy

   1. ____________________

   2. ____________________

   3. ____________________

   4. ____________________

   5. ____________________

4. What five things would you recommend a manager do to show more empathy for X'ers?

   1. ____________________

   2. ____________________

   3. ____________________

   4. ____________________

   5. ____________________

7

DIRECT COMMUNICATION

TOP TEN REASONS FOR MANAGER-X'ER COMMUNICATION GAPS

10. Consistency in management's approach is more the exception than the rule.
9. Glorified performance review system provides for a total of one hour of employee feedback per year.
8. "Soon" means promised for January, happening in late May.
7. Quality standards defined by whomever is in charge at that moment.
6. Mind games and double messages are managers' way of keeping X'ers on their toes.
5. Organizational politics dictate what *really* needs to get done.
4. New employee orientation held after two months on the job.
3. "Big picture" is best-kept management secret.
2. Last time written job descriptions were updated was in 1972.
1. Wait a minute, did you say *written* job descriptions?

Personnel Department "Cynics"
Buffalo, NY

SPELLING IT OUT

"Good communication means having the impact you intended to have, that is, Intent equals Impact. In other words, good communication...is clear and precise. The speaker tries to clarify the intent of his message by stating exactly what he is thinking, wanting, or feeling. He does not assume the listener 'knows' what is going on [inside] his head; he tells the listener so that the listener doesn't have to guess or mind read."

John Gottman, Cliff Notarius, Jonni Gonso and Howard Markman in *A Couple's Guide to Communication*

The X-Generation yearns for managers who are straightforward and apolitical. **Direct Communication, the fifth and final point of the NAKED Model, mandates that X'er-manager interactions are clear, concise, expressive, and immediate.** Both parties have important responsibilities in this process that require conscious awareness and commitment to improving the climate of their mutual working environment.

Members of the X-workforce need structure as well as room to breathe and make on-the-job decisions. In essence, Direct Communication serves as a check and balance on Necessary Freedom. This benefits both managers and X'ers alike. Knowing the rules of the game curbs the chances that X'ers will drift beyond acceptable limits when they are granted higher levels of autonomy. It relieves managers from some of the natural tensions and premature remorse associated with giving up degrees of power or control.

Direct Communication for X'ers, meanwhile, keeps them goal-directed, motivated, and implicitly on task. An example of a management practice which helps elicit this positive response involves letting members of the X-workforce know the precise performance outcomes upon which they will be evaluated. Managers can satisfy X'ers hunger for the "big picture" by giving them a clear snapshot of what is expected.

Regarding the specifics of Direct Communication, managers can equip X'ers with a sample copy of the employee performance appraisal form for their company and go over the process with them. A variation on this theme is to hold a simulation session where members of the X-Generation get a realistic preview of the actual performance review procedure. In addition, new employee orientation programs — initiated *on* the day X'ers start their jobs, not two to 10 weeks afterward — assist in clarifying mutual expectations from the outset.

Other ways in which managers can promote Direct Communication with X'ers include agreeing on project check-back points and deadlines, specifying performance standards and expectations, spelling out disciplinary procedures, designating appropriate channels of communication, identifying available resources, delineating opportunities for advancement, and defining the company's mission. The primary objectives in each of these scenarios are to ensure clarity and eliminate guesswork for both managers and the X-workforce.

Ongoing consistency in managers' actions and policies is also an essential part of Direct Communication. Invariably, "saying one thing then doing another" destroys credibility and morale with the X-Generation. X'ers are inspired by managers who walk their talk. They want managers upon whom they can depend. X'ers' perceptions of their managers can determine whether or not they will stay at a job, and how hard they will work while they are there.

The role of X'ers in the Direct Communication process is to ensure that it actually happens. Whether this involves asking for written job descriptions or setting up time to discuss performance expectations and goals with their managers, members of the X-workforce must take responsibility for staying informed. Gaining a clear understanding of what their managers need them to do in turn makes their jobs more enjoyable and stress free.

THE NAKED CONTRACT

> *"'...You see, in most organizations when you ask people what they do and then ask their boss, all too often you get two different lists. In fact, in some organizations I've worked in, any relationship between what I thought my job responsibilities were and what my boss thought they were, was purely coincidental. And then I would get in trouble for not doing something I didn't even think was my job.'"*
>
> Excerpt from *The One Minute Manager*
> by Ken Blanchard and Spencer Johnson

The Naked Contract is a simple tool for spelling out Direct Communication with the X-workforce. It is the vehicle by which managers and X'ers can bridge communication gaps about performance expectations. Structurally, the Naked Contract draws out responsibilities for both individual X'ers and their managers as the two sets of information mutually relate (see Figure 4). In certain cases, the Naked Contract may take the form of a verbal agreement.

In formulating the Naked Contract, both managers and X'ers provide input. While the core of the agreement may be based on pre-established performance objectives, there is still room for modifications or additions as productivity requirements change. Because the Naked Contract reflects the joint interests of managers and X'ers, it needs to be fully acceptable to each party. Signing a hard copy of this agreement helps to assure dual commitment. Subsequently, it becomes a distinctive frame of reference for managers and X'ers alike, giving them a substantial document to fall back on in discrepancies or ambiguities about expected job performance.

The Naked Contract (sample form)

Name of Company: ______________________________

Name of X'er: ______________________________

Name of Manager: ______________________________

Date: ______________________________

X'er Performance Objectives (Responsibilities/Goals):

1. ______________________________
2. ______________________________
3. ______________________________
4. ______________________________
5. ______________________________
6. ______________________________

Manager Responsibilities in Helping X'er Meet Stated Objectives:

1. ______________________________
2. ______________________________
3. ______________________________
4. ______________________________
5. ______________________________
6. ______________________________

Signed: ______________________________

Figure 4

NAKED SUCCESS: PROFILE OF A **JIFFY LUBE** X'ER

Company: **JIFFY LUBE INTERNATIONAL, INC.**
Industry: Automotive - Quick Lube
Headquarters: Houston, Texas

Key Facts: In 1990, most of Jiffy Lube International was acquired by Pennzoil Company. From 1991, Jiffy Lube began to buy back service centers from many of its larger franchisees, increasing the number of corporate-owned and operated stores. Also in 1991, Pennzoil completed its purchase of the remaining shares of the company. By the end of 1994, 1,141 Jiffy Lubes were open throughout the world, and the company set new systemwide sales records at $608 million — an increase of $68 million, or 13%, from the previous year. The number of cars serviced in 1994 also made a significant climb from 1993, from 16 to 17.7 million. Recently, Jiffy Lube and Sears Merchandise Group have agreed to open Jiffy Lube units in Sears Auto Centers across the United States. Jiffy Lube prides itself in customer service and consistency in operating standards. Jiffy Lube has rolled out its Signature Service program to address its mission statement theme of quality service for every customer.

> *"My supervisor is up front when there are problems, but he doesn't just back you out the door and 'let you have it.' Instead we sit down, discuss things, then move on."*

Name: Jose
Title: Store Manager
Age: 23

Tenure/History: Jose came to South Florida Lubes, a growing franchise of Jiffy Lube, at age 19. He began working as a lower bay technician, then got promoted after one year to upper bay technician. By age 21, Jose was moved up to the assistant manager position. Now at 23 years old, Jose has been with Jiffy Lube for five years at the same location. He has been the proud manager of that store for almost two years. Recently, Jose starred in a local Jiffy Lube television spot shown throughout South Florida.

Motivating Things About His Job: *"Everything is very clearly communicated. I know exactly what I need to do. We have the Jiffy Lube '14 Point Service' which makes every customer's experience consistent, fast and thorough. Our performance goals are spelled out to the letter. We have regular manager meetings with the franchise owners themselves to increase communication."*

Motivating Things About His Boss: *"I know that I can talk openly to management — any time of the day. They even give us their home numbers. Why? So we can communicate <u>when</u> we need to, not a week later. They are very clear about this. They want to work together to solve problems."*

What Keeps Him From Leaving: *"When Benny, my supervisor, or even Dan, the franchise president, need to address an issue with me, they don't just say, 'Hey, here's what's wrong, now go fix it.' They like to ask, 'How can we help you?' The feedback is direct, but it is a process that I am part of. They want to communicate with me, not come down on me. <u>That</u> is what makes me come to work each day with a good attitude."*

Most Memorable "Naked Moment": *"These guys don't just ask for my views, they listen. I gave them feedback on what I see is a big issue in our multicultural surroundings. A significant number of our area customers speak Spanish, many as a first language. I suggested it was high time we start doing bilingual marketing. Dan and Benny knew it made sense. Two weeks later we have flyers and coupons in Spanish!"*

LETTING 'EM KNOW WHERE THEY STAND

"There are three important rules for giving feedback. It has to be immediate, honest, and supportive. Immediate means as soon as you fully understand the communication... Putting your feedback off, even a few hours, makes it much less valuable. Honest means your real reaction... You don't have to cut somebody up to give your reaction. In fact, brutality is rarely honest. Your feedback should be honest and supportive. You can be gentle, saying what you need to say without causing damage or defensiveness.... 'think there's a real possibility that you've made a mistake' is more supportive than 'You've been a fool.'"

Matthew McKay, Martha Davis,
and Patrick Fanning in *Messages: The Communication Skills Book*

If feedback is the "breakfast of champions," as Ken Blanchard and Spencer Johnson state in *The One Minute Manager,* then X'ers are champs with enormous appetites. Members of the X-Generation like to know where they stand. Supplying X'ers with feedback as part of Direct Communication provides an instant reality check on the quality of their performance. It also allows managers to confront them on behaviors interpreted as slacking off or whining.

The manner in which feedback is delivered is critical to the achievement of positive outcomes. To be truly effective, managers must consider the following guidelines for giving feedback to the X-Generation: ensure feedback is related to work performance and the bottom line, make sure it is specific and concise so X'ers know *exactly* which behaviors to address, offer both positive and negative feedback, initiate it immediately after behavior for greatest impact, show warmth and professionalism, use facts instead of opinions, provide it on a regular basis, summarize overall impressions, and be aware of nonverbal behavior. Tact is equally important. X'ers get quickly turned off if they perceive that managers are patronizing or condescending to them.

Members of the X-workforce appreciate being included in the Direct Communication feedback loop. They want to know *why* something they have done is "incorrect" or *why* a particular procedure they must follow is set up in a certain way. Some managers call this whining, yet it is X'ers' way of seeking closure on issues they are trying to understand.

Additionally, X'ers like it when managers come to *them* and ask for feedback. A tangible way for managers to facilitate this process is to schedule weekly or bimonthly staff meetings to solicit X'er input. As an alternative, they can create a task force to address issues specifically relevant to the X-workforce. In such cases, X'ers have to do more than simply give their fair share of feedback to managers. While it is important that they assert their views and identify areas in which their expectations are not being met, they need to be *receptive* to Direct Communication feedback as well. They must make a concerted effort to stay open-minded instead of taking the defensive.

NAKED SUCCESS: PROFILE OF A **UNITED AIRLINES** X'ER

Company: **UNITED AIRLINES**
Industry: Airline
Headquarters: Chicago, Illinois

Key Facts: On July 12, 1994, United Airlines became the largest majority employee-owned company in the world. It currently has over 78,000 employees. The "friendly skies" of United now span five continents, 30 countries, and three territories with service to 104 domestic and 39 international airports worldwide. In addition, 184 airports are served by United Express partners. Each day, United's 2,200 flights carry approximately 203,000 customers. Covering a broad network throughout North America, South America, Asia, Central America, Australia, New Zealand, and Europe, United is one of the world's largest passenger airlines. It is also one of the largest cargo carriers in the world, flying over two billion cargo ton miles in 1994. In October 1994, United launched its new "airline within an airline" Shuttle by United. This low-price short-haul flight service was then expanded from 184 to 378 daily departures. United also is proud to be the largest tenant at Denver International Airport, the first major new airport built in the United States in more than 20 years.

> *"I want to be with this company as long as I can. I really like it here. United is a very professional, well-run organization."*

Name: Vanessa
Title: Flight Attendant
Age: 27

Tenure/History: Vanessa, a resident of Taipei, started at age 23 in the airline industry working as a flight attendant. When United Airlines opened a base in Taipei two years later, she was quickly hired by the company. Upon becoming a United Airlines flight attendant, Vanessa was soon given additional responsibilities to help facilitate the smooth flow of the Taipei operations. Her hard work and leadership skills were formally recognized when she was selected as one of only two 1994 Rookies of the Year. Vanessa is extremely grateful for what she calls "the first award of her career."

Motivating Things About Her Job: *"I like working for United Airlines because they treat you like a human being. You can use your own judgment as long as you are representing the mutual best interest of the passengers and the company. We have clear procedures, but you can do whatever it takes to <u>enhance</u> service."*

Motivating Things About Her Boss: *"My supervisor demands excellence and has very high standards. But she is <u>consistent</u> and <u>clear</u>. She has the same requirements for herself. She truly 'walks her talk' — it is in her attitude and behavior. This makes me see her as being fair. She is very direct, but you respect her because you know she is right. She keeps you honest and on task. She also has a good sense of humor, even when you do something wrong."*

<u>What Keeps Her From Leaving:</u> *"When Tien-Tien, my supervisor, sees improvement, she gives me feedback <u>right away</u> and says, 'Keep it up.' I also feel comfortable giving her feedback, both good and bad. It is usually in our casual conversations — it does not have to be planned. I am very at ease when talking to her. I do not feel inferior like other bosses make you feel. We are like family, and we are friends."*

Most Memorable "Naked Moment": *"When I won the 1994 Rookie of the Year Award, the company flew me to Chicago for a big awards luncheon. It was terrific. But one of the most special things was when my supervisor, Tien-Tien, said to me, 'United Airlines is lucky to have someone like you. It is a tremendous loss for the other airlines.'"*

IT'S HOW YOU SAY IT

> *"...Gut-level communication (emotional openness and honesty) must never imply a judgment of the other ....For example, if I were to say to you, 'I am ill at ease with you,' I have been emotionally honest and at the same time have not implied in the least that it is your fault that I am ill at ease with you. ...If I were to say to you that I feel angry or hurt by something you have done or said, I have not judged you."*
>
> John Powell in *Why Am I Afraid to Tell You Who I Am?*

Whether spelling out behavioral expectations or giving performance feedback, assertiveness and tact are deep-seated principles of Direct Communication. These interpersonal strategies help separate self-expression from other-blaming. Through their usage, working relationships between managers and the X-workforce are strengthened, energized, and positively reinforced.

Keeping X'ers off the defensive while delivering Direct Communication is not always easy. One intervention managers can use to avoid sounding like they are attacking or blaming X'ers is called an "I-message." According to Ron Adler and Neil Towne in *Looking Out/Looking In, "'I' language describes the speaker's reaction to the other's behavior without making any judgments about its worth."* Complete I-messages, in the context of Naked Management, have four parts: (a) the speaker's feeling, (b) the recipient's exact behavior that caused the speaker to feel that way, (c) the consequences of that behavior for the speaker, and, (d) what the speaker would like the recipient to do or refrain from doing in order to achieve problem resolution.

An example of when an I-message can be used is found in the following communication from a manager to an X'er staff member whose mistake cost his company a small loss in revenue:

"Look how you screwed up. You're incompetent! One more stupid mistake like that and you're fired."

If an I-message were substituted, the exchange might go as follows:

> *"It both upsets and angers me [manager's feeling] that you did not double check your work this morning [X'er's exact behavior]. It cost us $20 [consequences of X'er's behavior]. I need you to be more*

accountable in following the transaction procedures we have already reviewed if you want to continue working here [what manager needs X'er to do for problem resolution]."

Through the use of this I-message, the manager projected honesty and tact and took responsibility for her own feelings and emotions. She explained why she felt the way she did and spelled out exactly what she needed to have happen. Her Direct Communication was neither aggressive nor provoking. When X'ers are spoken to in this professional, caring manner, they are more apt to listen and respond favorably to feedback.

By the same token, the X-Generation must use I-messages in their Direct Communication with managers. The key for both X'ers and managers is to adapt the basic structure of this technique to their own style, then actively practice it until it becomes fluent and natural. Mastery of I-messages not only improves job satisfaction, but breaks down interpersonal barriers to reaching bottom-line performance objectives.

NAKED CHECKLIST: DIRECT COMMUNICATION

Fulfillment of each of the following tasks is a key aspect of implementing Naked Management as it relates to this chapter. The listed items for managers and X'ers may be added to or revised to fit individual work environments or company policies.

For Managers:

___ 1. ***Use Direct Communication to ensure your management style is viewed by the X-workforce as honest, straightforward, and apolitical.*** Interactions with X'ers must be clear, concise, expressive and immediate.

___ 2. ***Give X'ers structure by providing them with the rules of the game.*** This will complement — not compete with — their Necessary Freedom.

___ 3. ***Spell out performance standards, goals, and expectations for X'ers.*** Equip them with a sample copy of the company's performance appraisal form and go over it with them via simulation. Promptly initiate new X'er orientation programs and be consistent in your actions and policies. Clarify X'er responsibilities in verbal and written communications and through experiential activities.

___ 4. ***Administer feedback to let X'ers know where they stand.*** Make certain it is related to work performance and the bottom line. It needs to be specific and concise, formal and informal, positive as well as negative, immediate, frequent, warm, professional, and factual. Include X'ers in the process by scheduling regular staff meetings or creating a task force on X-workforce issues.

___ 5. ***Say what is on your mind with an I-message.*** Include (a) the speaker's feeling, (b) the recipient's exact behavior that caused the speaker to feel that way, (c) the consequences of that behavior for the speaker, and, (d) what the speaker would like the recipient to do or refrain from doing in order to achieve problem resolution.

___ 6. ***Develop and sign a Naked Contract with each of your X'ers.*** The final agreement must reflect your joint interests and needs to be fully acceptable to both of you. Check that you mutually understand and are willing to abide by the specifications of this Naked Contract.

For X'ers:

___ 1. ***Ensure that managers spell out performance standards, goals, and expectations.*** Ask for written job descriptions and set up time to discuss work objectives with them. Stay informed and see to it that you have a clear understanding of what you need to do.

___ 2. ***Do more than simply give your fair share of feedback to managers.*** While this is important, you need to be especially *receptive* to feedback as well. Make a concerted effort to be nondefensive, mature, and open-minded.

___ 3. ***Incorporate I-messages into your Direct Communication with managers.*** Actively practice this technique until it becomes fluent.

___ 4. ***Develop and sign a Naked Contract with your manager.*** Make certain that you understand and are willing to abide by its specifications.

X'ERCISE 7: CLEARING THE AIR

DIRECTIONS

The following items are designed to help you assess your strategy for putting the NAKED Model component "**D**irect Communication" into practice. Write your answers in the spaces provided or on a separate sheet of paper. Then, discuss your responses with other managers and/or X'ers.

1a. **(for managers only):**
How good of a job would your X'ers say you do at providing Direct Communication (spelling things out, giving feedback, being tactfully assertive)?
  a. excellent
  b. fair
  c. poor

1b. **(for X'ers only):**
How good of a job does your manager do at providing Direct Communication (spelling things out, giving feedback, being tactfully assertive)?
  a. excellent
  b. fair
  c. poor

2. List three *specific* examples of how you are successful at providing Direct Communication:

   1. ______________________________

   2. ______________________________

   3. ______________________________

3. List three *specific* examples of how you could improve at providing Direct Communication:

   1. ______________________________

   2. ______________________________

   3. ______________________________

4. Think of a time when the way in which you verbally expressed yourself to an X'er (or to your manager) may have been construed as "blaming." Write down that "blame-message" in the space below, followed by the corresponding "I-message" that would be more appropriate and effective.

   Blame Message: ______________________________

   I-Message: ______________________________

5. Develop a draft of your own Naked Contract that realistically can be implemented in your personal work environment. Use the sample form in Figure 4 as a guide.

8

NAKED PROOF

Top Ten Sure-Fire Ways to Make Naked Management Fail

10. Disregard everything you have read in the last seven chapters.
9. Try to convince yourself that the X-Generation is simply a passing marketing fad which has no implications for the workplace.
8. Insist that it really doesn't matter how you treat X'ers anyway — they *need* their jobs too bad to just quit.
7. Launch Naked Management, then do nothing more than give it lip scrvicc.
6. Get caught up on the word "naked" — have a special subcommittee look into it over the next couple of months.
5. Insist that you were much happier *before* Naked Management.
4. Agree to implement the NAKED Model only if it means you don't have to *do* anything.
3. Stay convinced that X'ers respond better to ball-and-chain tactics.
2. Put Naked Management on the back burner because it interferes with your company's "program of the month" rotisserie training schedule.
1. Remark to X'ers, *"Finally, a five-point plan that will keep you little brats from whining so much."*

Enlightened Naked Managers
San Diego, CA

WHATEVER YOU DO, DON'T MEASURE IT

> *"...it would be unrealistic to pretend that most programs are either based upon appropriate needs assessment or that these programs are examined to determine the degree to which they achieve their objectives. Unfortunately, most organizations do not have information available to determine the utility of their own instructional programs. Their techniques remain unevaluated, except for the high esteem with which they are regarded by training personnel.... Yet, when evaluation studies are completed, it is often found that the techniques are not achieving the desired results, and in many cases the evaluation could provide clues to the modifications necessary to enable the program to work."*
>
> Irwin Goldstein in
> *Training in Organizations*

Measuring the effectiveness of the five NAKED Model components is just as important as knowing how to use them. Both managers and X'ers want to see progress and improvement. Naked Proof — the tracking of Naked Management as it relates to bottom-line objectives — represents a critical aspect of implementing the NAKED Model.

The pressing need to anchor Naked Management outcomes to performance standards requires managers and X'ers to review the Naked Contract (see previous chapter) they mutually created and upon which they agreed. Some examples of bottom-line indicators used to establish Naked Proof include X-workforce turnover, productivity (e.g., generated sales), morale, job satisfaction, attendance, absenteeism, and goal attainment. Specifically looking at the issue of turnover, Robert Mathis and John Jackson, in their text *Human Resource Management,* write the following:

> *Turnover occurs when employees leave an organization and have to be replaced. It can be a very costly problem, one with a major impact on productivity. One firm had a turnover rate of more than 120% per year! It cost the company $1.5 million a year in lost productivity, increased training time, increased employee selection time, lost work efficiency, and other indirect costs....Lengthy training times, interrupted schedules, overtime for others, mistakes, and not having knowledgeable employees in place are some of the frustrations associated with excessive turnover.*

Generally, the costs associated with replacing just one member of the X-Generation can range from several thousand dollars to more than $10,000, depending on the industry and position level of the X'er. Assessed in these figures are factors such as advertising and recruitment, interviewing, hiring, orientation, classroom and on-the-job training, benefits, paperwork, and all of the hours logged by each of the managers, trainers, and administrative personnel who are involved in these processes. A price tag is attached to the aftermath of an X'er leaving as well, i.e., being understaffed and having "ripple effects" where morale drops and additional employees consider quitting.

The overwhelming implication is that managers who believe the X-workforce is an easily discardable resource pay an expensive price. It is the reason managers need to evaluate the application of NAKED Model components through Naked Proof. If positive results in X'er performance can be demonstrated over time, then even the most skeptical managers may glean a fresh perspective on engaging in Naked Management practices with the X-Generation.

NAKED SUCCESS: PROFILE OF A **TULANE UNIVERSITY** X'ER

Organization: **TULANE UNIVERSITY**
Industry: Education
Headquarters: New Orleans, Louisiana

Key Facts: Tulane was founded in 1834 as the Medical College of Louisiana, then as Tulane University in 1884. Its enrollment exceeds 11,000 students from all 50 states and 80 foreign countries. There are 704 full-time faculty members. The main campus covers 110 acres of uptown New Orleans. In total, Tulane has 11 schools and colleges including the Paul Tulane College of Arts and Sciences, Newcomb College, the School of Architecture, the School of Engineering, the A.B. Freeman School of Business, the Graduate School, the School of Law, the School of Medicine, the School of Public Health and Tropical Medicine, the School of Social Work, and the University College. Tulane is ranked in the top quartile of the nation's most highly selective private universities. Its SAT scores average more than 25% above the national average. It is ranked among the top 25 private American universities in research and development funding, according to the National Science Foundation. Tulane also has an intensive sports program for men and women.

> *"I love my job, and I love where I live. My boss is a great guy to work for, too. I'd have to say it's a unique situation."*

Name: Lenny
Title: Assistant Athletic Director
Age: 29

Tenure/History: Lenny started working in the athletic department at Tulane University while attending college at Loyola. At age 17, he was a student assistant to the sports information director, and continued in that position for five years. At age 24, he returned and was hired on as the associate sports information director. Within two years, he was promoted to sports information director. Only three years later, Lenny was moved up to the position of assistant athletic director. In total, Lenny's career at Tulane already exceeds 10 years at age 29.

Motivating Things About His Job: *"It's a different challenge every day. My position is very non-desk-oriented, which I like. The work is at the sporting events. I love the constant change of pace. I also enjoy the fact that I feel completely competent and comfortable at my job. I am trusted to make my own decisions and do what I do best."*

Motivating Things About His Boss: *"Ian used to have my position at one time. He's done everything I do now. So more than anything else, he can really relate to what I'm going through. It allows us to have a common bond. Ian also does a great job of giving me the space I need. He's a hands-off manager, which is critical. In his eyes, I was hired for a reason. He lets me do my job, so he can have time to do his."*

What Keeps Him From Leaving: *"This is home, both literally and metaphorically. I have lived in New Orleans all of my life. I've been in this department all of my working life. Everyone knows me and respects me. I've built a strong foundation for myself. It's like a comfort zone. I have no good reason to leave. I can't even remember ever sending out a résumé."*

Most Memorable "Naked Moment": *"During the men's basketball NCAA Tournament this year I got the chicken pox. It was one of our busiest and most exciting times, yet here I was, unable to travel. My boss just told me not to worry — 'he'll take care of it.' You know, even in my frustration, I was never worried. It's nice to fully trust your boss and know he's on your team."*

STAYING ON TRACK: THE NAKED TRACKING SYSTEM

"...in reality, evaluation is ongoing during every step of the process. This perpetual monitoring provides the feedback and input necessary for continuous improvement. It also allows us to track progress and measure against established milestones. It is important to build yardsticks into the system so worthwhile results are tracked on a regular basis. We firmly believe in the adages: 'you get what you inspect, not what you expect' and 'you can't manage what you don't measure.'"

Jay Spechler in *Managing Quality in America's Most Admired Companies*

In addition to the Naked Checklists and chapter X'ercises found in this book, the Naked Tracking System (see sample form in Figure 5) serves as a useful measurement tool for tracking the ongoing effectiveness of Naked Management. A key element of this instrument for obtaining Naked Proof is that it is fully adaptable. It can be tailored to any work setting and changed to reflect modifications in performance goals. By working together on its design, managers and X'ers can jointly maintain its continued usage.

One of the first steps in using the Naked Tracking System form is identifying the specific performance objectives which will be measured (e.g., productivity, morale, turnover). This information can be adapted from the Naked Contract. Performance objectives need to be listed on separate Naked Tracking System forms.

Next, the barriers to achieving these objectives have to be determined and recorded in the appropriate space on every form. As a result, managers and X'ers are alerted to obstacles which potentially preclude bottom-line goal attainment. NAKED Model strategies (see Naked Checklists) can then be used to develop an action plan for working through or eliminating these performance barriers. The resulting action steps must be listed in the identified area on the Naked Tracking System form.

Naked Tracking System (sample form)

Performance Objective:

1. ______________________________

Performance Barrier(s):

1. ______________________________

2. ______________________________

3. ______________________________

Action Step(s):

1. ______________________________

2. ______________________________

3. ______________________________

4. ______________________________

5. ______________________________

Naked Proof (performance outcomes, how they are measured and follow-up):

1. ______________________________

2. ______________________________

3. ______________________________

Figure 5

Finally, performance outcomes (e.g., generated savings, profits, incurred costs, benefits), the methods by which they were measured and any follow-up procedures need to be entered under the "Naked Proof" heading of the form. For this effort to be maximally effective, it is important that managers and X'ers adhere to a mutually agreed upon time schedule (e.g., every day, once a week, twice per month) for reviewing problems and progress, as well as new or modified performance objectives which require additional Naked Tracking forms. Both parties must keep a sequential file of all Naked Tracking System forms they mutually generate to preserve a true and easily accessible performance history.

LIP SERVICE 101

> *"...all too often seen in companies: the lip service disaster and the gimmicks disaster....The lip service disaster is arguably the worse of the two. Almost every management we've been around says that people are important — vital, in fact. But having said that, they then don't pay much attention to their people. In fact, they probably don't even realize their omissions. 'People issues take up all my time,' is the typical rejoinder. What they often really mean is, 'This business would be so easy if it weren't for people.'"*
>
> Tom Peters and Robert Waterman, Jr. in
> *In Search of Excellence*

Lip service is a prime culprit in most contexts of failure in the workplace. It can single-handedly make the Naked Tracking System a worthless tool. If managers and X'ers want positive Naked Proof, they must truly commit to the process of Naked Management and make it a top priority. Otherwise, the effort is meaningless and will be sabotaged before it even begins.

Common situations which can lead to NAKED Model lip service include the "shotgun approach," where Naked Management is nothing more than the "training program of the month," replaced in 30 days by the latest topic management gurus consider popular; the "knee-jerk reaction," when company leaders spontaneously make up their minds that Naked Management will be rolled out the following day, regardless of the implicit needs or readiness of the organization; too much hype, such that a major emphasis is put on bells, whistles, and buzzwords instead of on the practical concerns of integrating Naked Management into the organizational culture; poor timing (e.g., introducing Naked Management in the middle of a chaotic or busy period); lack of planning or preparation; "spotted history," meaning past attempts to enhance management practices have been typically unsuccessful; and unrealistic expectations, characterized by empty promises. Each of these scenarios can breed enough resistance and negativity to kill Naked Management on the spot.

Managers and X'ers must together create an organizational climate which is more conducive to welcoming and accepting Naked Management as a lasting institution. Proactive measures consist of doing thorough needs assessments, obtaining input and buy-in *prior* to process implementation, evaluating the timing for launching Naked Management, setting realistic expectations, *gradually* phasing in Naked Management over a predetermined period of time, giving Naked Management its own positive identity, and positioning it so that it will be perceived as distinctly separate from other company initiatives.

NAKED SUCCESS: PROFILE OF AN **OFFICE DEPOT** X'ER

Company: **OFFICE DEPOT**
Industry: Office Products and Supplies
Headquarters: Delray Beach, Florida

Key Facts: Office Depot is the world's largest office products retailer, operating more than 500 stores throughout the United States and Canada. Total net sales for 1995 were $5.3 billion — a 50% increase over sales in 1993. By the end of 1996, Office Depot will have approximately 580 stores, with 80 new stores per year planned for 1997 and 1998. The company operates a national delivery network to serve the office supply needs of medium- and large-size businesses. This operation includes 24 customer service centers/delivery warehouses and 70 sales offices. Office Depot has had four stock splits since 1989. Office Depot's mission is to be the "most successful office products company in the world." The company's superior management and motivated associate team is highly committed to this goal. The team spirit at Office Depot is unprecedented; people are very proud to be a part of the great things that are happening there. Office Depot prides itself on its keen ability to adapt, lead, and thrive on change in a fast-paced and highly competitive market environment.

> *"It's fun to bring people into this company and watch them succeed and grow. As a stockholder, I take a lot of pride in Office Depot and the welfare of my co-associates."*

Name: Dale
Title: Senior Human Resources Representative
Age: 28

Tenure/History: At age 21, Dale started in public accounting at a major national firm. She soon switched to a human resources role within the accounting industry, and at 27 was hired by Office Depot to do professional recruiting. With her specialized background, she has taken on major responsibilities in the recruitment and hiring of all finance personnel at the Office Depot Support Center, which employs over 1,200 associates. Dale has not only excelled but has shown her multifaceted talents as a human resources generalist. She was promoted into a senior generalist role supporting the Southeast Region retail division.

Motivating Things About Her Job: *"Office Depot is hard work integrated with fun. I am actually happy to come to work each day. There is* <u>*balance*</u> *here. It is a caring environment full of new challenges every day. When they hire you here, they are looking for confidence and ability, not to 'fill' a position. The focus is on where you're going, not on where you've been."*

Motivating Things About Her Boss: *"My boss, Joann, really knows how to motivate me. She provides constant challenge, knowing that I will rise to the occasion and embrace it. She gives me the opportunity to create and to prove myself. She helps me grow through nonjudgmental feedback. She is a great teacher, definitely the best coach I have ever had."*

What Keeps Her From Leaving: *"Hierarchy is almost nonexistent here. If a senior executive needs to talk to you, he or she will call you or see you directly. The pyramid is flat; the red tape is cut. Our CEO will not tolerate it any other way. The prevailing message from management is, 'We care about you — as an associate and as a person.' This positiveness spills over into our productivity. The financial results and great morale prove it."*

Most Memorable "Naked Moment": *"I was with Joann at a recent meeting with top management. When it was her turn to present, she said, 'Dale will run our portion of the meeting.' She had the total confidence in me to let me represent our team. She knows I will give her a strong return on her investment. Most bosses present your work* <u>*for*</u> *you — not my boss."*

THE RETURN ON INVESTMENT

> *"...Although this effort [embracing diversity] will take energy and commitment, it will result in significant long-term advantages for those organizations willing to make the necessary investment. Foremost among these long-term advantages will be:*
>
> - *The full utilization of the organization's human capital...*
> - *Reduced interpersonal conflict...*
> - *Enhanced work relationships...*
> - *A shared organizational vision and increased commitment...*
> - *Greater innovation and flexibility...*
> - *Improved productivity..."*
>
> Marilyn Loden and Judy Rosener in *Workforce America!: Managing Employee Diversity as a Vital Resource*

The X-workforce's productivity, morale, and loyalty are immutably tied to Naked Management. A team atmosphere and an aura of synergy quickly evolve when the NAKED Model is put into daily practice. It stimulates X'ers' desire to work hard and promotes their sense of job commitment. In the end, managers spend less time feeling frustrated, angry, or helpless in their interactions with members of the X-Generation. When X'ers do their share to bolster the effectiveness of the Naked Management, they become valued contributors instead of unworthy complainers.

Naked Management is a lesson in embracing diversity. It is the unsolicited answer to the X-Crisis, and the impetus for bringing winning change to a workplace that so desperately needs it. Ultimately, it is the golden key which frees managers and X'ers from gridlock, and the silver chain which pulls them out of the mud. Respect — not sympathy — for each other's inherent differences, unique perspectives, and individual values fosters positive organizational climates where managers and X'ers can productively, even happily, work together.

NAKED CHECKLIST: **NAKED** PROOF

Fulfillment of each of the following tasks is a key aspect of implementing Naked Management as it relates to this chapter. The listed items for managers and X'ers may be added to or revised to fit individual work environments or company policies.

For Managers and X'ers:

_____ 1. ***Make Naked Proof — the tracking of Naked Management as it relates to bottom-line objectives — a vital part of NAKED Model implementation.*** Monitor the workplace effectiveness of the hands-on strategies you adopt.

_____ 2. ***Combat the conditions which lead to lip service.*** Try to eliminate the occurrence of situations characterized by the presence of the shotgun approach, the knee-jerk reaction, too much hype, poor timing, lack of planning or preparation, spotted history, and unrealistic expectations.

_____ 3. ***Set up an organizational climate conducive to welcoming and accepting Naked Management as a lasting institution.*** Be proactive by facilitating needs assessments, obtaining input and buy-in*prior* to implementation, evaluating timing, setting realistic expectations, gradually phasing in Naked Management over a predetermined period of time, giving Naked Management its own positive identity, and positioning it as distinctly separate from other company initiatives.

_____ 4. ***Anchor performance outcomes to measurable objectives.*** Collect data on turnover, productivity (e.g., generated sales), morale, job satisfaction, attendance, absenteeism, goal attainment, and overall financial performance.

_____ 5. ***Keep in mind that losing even one X'er is very expensive.*** Consistently apply the NAKED Model to reduce X-workforce turnover.

_____ 6. ***Stay on track by using the Naked Tracking System.*** Develop this tool as a joint manager-X'er project to provide ongoing Naked Proof. Tailor it to your work setting and change it to reflect day-to-day developments or modifications in your performance goals.

X'ERCISE 8: ON THE RIGHT TRACK

DIRECTIONS

The following items are designed to help you make "Naked Proof" a vital part of your implementation of the NAKED model. Write your answers in the spaces provided or on a separate sheet of paper. Then, discuss your responses with other managers and/or X'ers.

1a. **(for managers only):**
How good of a job would your X'ers say you and the company do at providing Naked Proof (i.e., measurement and tracking) of performance, progress and the results of implemented programs?
a. excellent
b. fair
c. poor

1b. **(for X'ers only):**
How good of a job does your manager and the company do at providing Naked Proof (i.e., measurement and tracking) of performance, progress and the results of implemented programs?
a. excellent
b. fair
c. poor

2. List three *specific* examples of when you experience, or are guilty of, lip service at work:

1. ______________________________

2. ______________________________

3. ______________________________

3. List three *specific* examples of how you and your company could improve at providing Naked Proof (i.e., measurement and tracking) of performance, progress and the results of implemented programs:

   1. ______________________________

   2. ______________________________

   3. ______________________________

4. List three *specific* examples of how you and your company do a good job of providing Naked Proof (i.e., measurement and tracking) of performance, progress and the results of implemented programs:

   1. ______________________________

   2. ______________________________

   3. ______________________________

5. Develop a draft of your own Naked Tracking System that realistically can be implemented in your personal work environment. Use the sample form in Figure 5 as a guide.

RECOMMENDED READING

Generation X: Tales for an Accelerated Culture by Douglas Coupland (St. Martin's)

The Healthy Company: Eight Strategies to Develop People, Productivity and Profits by Robert H. Rosen with Lisa Berger (Jeremy P. Tarcher/Perigree)

Leadership is an Art by Max DePree (Bantam Doubleday Dell)

Managing Quality in America's Most Admired Companies by Jay W. Spechler (Industrial Engineering and Management Press)

Moments of Truth: New Strategies for Today's Customer-Driven Economy by Jan Carlzon (Ballinger)

The 100 Best Companies to Work for in America by Robert Levering and Milton Moskowitz (Currency/Doubleday)

The One Minute Manager by Kenneth Blanchard and Spencer Johnson (Berkley)

1001 Ways to Reward Employees by Bob Nelson (Workman)

A Passion for Excellence: The Leadership Difference by Thomas J. Peters and Nancy Austin (Random House)

Service that Sells!: The Art of Profitable Hospitality by Jim Sullivan and Phil Roberts (Pencom)

The 7 Habits of Highly Effective People by Stephen R. Covey (Fireside/Simon & Schuster)

13th Generation: Abort, Retry, Ignore, Fail? by Neil Howe and Bill Strauss (Vintage)

Zapp! The Lightning of Empowerment by William C. Byham with Jeff Cox (Ballantine)

REFERENCES

Abromovitz, Hedy Gruenebaum, and Abromovitz, Les. *Bringing TQM on the QT to Your Organization.* Knoxville, TN: SPC Press, Inc., 1993, p. 203.

Adler, Ronald B., and Towne, Neil. *Looking Out/Looking In.* Fort Worth: Harcourt Brace Jovanovich College Publishers, 1993, pp. 109, 179.

Blanchard, Kenneth, and Johnson, Spencer. *The One Minute Manager.* New York: Berkley Books, 1982, pp. 27, 67.

Blanchard, Kenneth, Oncken, Jr., William, and Burrows, Hal. *The One Minute Manager Meets the Monkey.* New York: William Morrow and Company, Inc. 1989, p. 22.

Blanchard, Kenneth, and Peale, Norman Vincent. *The Power of Ethical Management.* New York: William Morrow and Company, Inc., 1988, p. 97.

Byham, William C. with Cox, Jeff. *Zapp! The Lightning of Empowerment.* New York: Ballantine Books, 1988, p. 55.

Carlzon, Jan. *Moments of Truth: New Strategies for Today's Customer-Driven Economy.* New York: Ballinger Publishing Company, 1987, p. 115.

Covey, Stephen R. *The 7 Habits of Highly Effective People.* New York: Fireside/Simon & Schuster, 1990, pp. 239, 241.

Cummings, Thomas G., and Huse, Edgar F. *Organization Development and Change.* St. Paul: West Publishing Company, 1989, p. 333.

DePree, Max. *Leadership is an Art.* New York: Bantam Doubleday Dell Publishing Group, Inc., 1989, pp. 104-105.

Filipczak, Bob. "It's Just a Job: Generation X at Work." *Training* (April, 1994), p. 24.

Gardner, John W. *Self-Renewal: The Individual and the Innovative Society.* New York: Harper & Row, Publishers, 1964, pp. 21-22.

Gibson, Jane Whitney. *The Supervisory Challenge: Principles and Practices.* New Jersey: Prentice Hall, 1995, p. 55.

Goldstein, Irwin L. *Training in Organizations: Needs Assessment, Development, and Evaluation.* Pacific Grove, CA: Brooks/Cole Publishing Company, 1986, p. 8.

Gottman, John, Notarius, Cliff, Gonso, Jonni and Markman, Howard. *A Couple's Guide to Communication.* Champaign, IL: Research Press, 1976, pp. 1-2.

Hammer, Michael, and Champy, James. *Reengineering the Corporation: A Manifesto for Business Revolution.* New York: HarperBusiness, 1993, p. 69.

Howe, Neil, and Strauss, Bill. *13th Generation: Abort, Retry, Ignore, Fail?* New York: Vintage Books, 1993, pp. 12-13.

Levering, Robert, and Moskowitz, Milton. *The 100 Best Companies to Work for in America.* New York: Currency/Doubleday, 1993, p. xiii.

Loden, Marilyn, and Rosener, Judy B. *Workforce America!: Managing Employee Diversity as a Vital Resource.* Burr Ridge, IL: Irwin Professional Publishing, 1991, p. 220.

Mathis, Robert L., and Jackson, John H. *Human Resource Management.* Minneapolis: West Publishing Corporation, 1994, p.102.

McKay, Matthew, Davis, Martha, and Fanning, Patrick. *Messages: The Communication Skills Book.* Oakland: New Harbinger Publications, 1992, p. 25.

Nelson, Bob. *1001 Ways to Reward Employees.* New York: Workman Publishing, 1994, p. xv.

O'Brien, Shannon P. "X Marks the Spot: How will Generation X Affect Your Firm?" *ALA News* (October/November, 1994), p. 30.

Peters, Thomas J., and Austin, Nancy. *A Passion for Excellence: The Leadership Difference.* New York: Random House, 1985, p. 201.

Peters, Thomas J., and Waterman, Robert H., Jr. *In Search of Excellence: Lessons from America's Best-Run Companies.* New York: Harper & Row, Publishers, 1982, p. 239.

Powell, John. *Why Am I Afraid to Tell You Who I Am?: Insights into Personal Growth.* Allen, TX: Tabor Publishing, 1969, pp. 57-58.

Ratan, Suneel. "Why Busters Hate Boomers." *Fortune* (October 4, 1993), p. 56-70.

Rogers, Carl R. *Freedom to Learn.* Columbus, OH: Charles E. Merrill Publishing Company, 1969, p. 105.

Rosen, Robert H. with Berger, Lisa. *The Healthy Company: Eight Strategies to Develop People, Productivity and Profits.* New York: Jeremy P. Tarcher/Perigree Books, 1991, pp. 31-32.

Sieghart, Mary Ann. "Talking about Generation X." *The Times* (December 5, 1994), Features section.

Spechler, Jay W. *Managing Quality in America's Most Admired Companies.* Norcross, GA: Industrial Engineering and Management Press, 1993, p. 49.

Steers, Richard M., and Porter, Lyman W. *Motivation and Work Behavior.* New York: McGraw-Hill, Inc., 1991, pp. 580, 581.

Sullivan, Jim, and Roberts, Phil. *Service that Sells!: The Art of Profitable Hospitality.* Denver: Pencom Press, 1991, pp.113-114.

Talking Heads. *"Road to Nowhere."* Appears on Little Creatures compact disc. Sire Records Company, 1985.

Wilkinson, Helen. "Slackers May Be Tomorrow's Winners At Work." *The Guardian* (November 30, 1994), Features section, p. 26.

Zill, Nicholas, and Robinson, John. "The Generation X Difference." *American Demographics* (April, 1995), p. 24.

NAKED MANAGEMENT SEMINARS, WORKSHOPS, AND SPEAKING ENGAGEMENTS

For all inquiries on Naked Management seminars, train-the-trainer workshops, and speaking engagement availability, write, call, fax, or E-mail Dr. Muchnick directly at:

People First Group
3111 University Drive, Suite 429
Coral Springs, FL 33065

Phone: (954) 344-1506
Fax: (954) 344-0462
E-mail: muchnicm@polaris.ncs.nova.edu